Creating a Strong Culture and Positive Climate in Schools

If there is one thing that school leaders need to get right, it is school culture. When they do, children learn more and colleagues have a stronger sense of purpose – they are more motivated and ultimately more fulfilled. Creating a strong culture and a positive climate requires an understanding of the complexity of school life and this begins by building knowledge. This book supports leaders to do just that.

Drawing on ideas from different domains, this insightful book reveals the role of concepts such as autonomy and trust in school improvement. Each chapter sets out the specific knowledge and expertise required by school leaders for great cultural leadership and offers practical examples and case studies to show how they can be applied in different school contexts.

Creating a Strong Culture and Positive Climate in Schools is an essential lens through which to examine the common problems faced by school leaders. It is invaluable reading for all those wanting to become more expert in school leadership and to better solve the everyday problems that arise from leading a school.

Nick Hart is the Executive Headteacher of the Alwyn and Courthouse Federation in Maidenhead. He has led in small schools and large schools; schools in a MAT and schools under local authority control; schools at the forefront of innovation and schools that required stabilising. Nick writes a well-established blog on education issues such as leadership, culture and curriculum design.

Creating a Strong Culture and Positive Climate in Schools

Building Knowledge to Bring About Improvement

Nick Hart

LONDON AND NEW YORK

Cover image: Getty images

First published 2022
by Routledge
4 Park Square, Milton Park, Abingdon, Oxon OX14 4RN

and by Routledge
605 Third Avenue, New York, NY 10158

Routledge is an imprint of the Taylor & Francis Group, an informa business

© 2022 Nick Hart

The right of Nick Hart to be identified as author of this work has been asserted in accordance with sections 77 and 78 of the Copyright, Designs and Patents Act 1988.

All rights reserved. No part of this book may be reprinted or reproduced or utilised in any form or by any electronic, mechanical, or other means, now known or hereafter invented, including photocopying and recording, or in any information storage or retrieval system, without permission in writing from the publishers.

Trademark notice: Product or corporate names may be trademarks or registered trademarks, and are used only for identification and explanation without intent to infringe.

British Library Cataloguing-in-Publication Data
A catalogue record for this book is available from the British Library

Library of Congress Cataloging-in-Publication Data
Names: Hart, Nick, 1982– author.
Title: Creating a strong culture and positive climate in schools: building knowledge to bring about improvement/Nick Hart.
Description: Abingdon, Oxon ; New York, NY : Routledge, 2023.
Identifiers: LCCN 2022009973 | ISBN 9781032168838 (hardback) | ISBN 9781032168845 (paperback) | ISBN 9781003250784 (ebook)
Subjects: LCSH: School environment. | School improvement programs. | Educational leadership. | School management and organization.
Classification: LCC LC210 .H37 2023 | DDC 370.15/8–dc23/eng/20220414
LC record available at https://lccn.loc.gov/2022009973

ISBN: 978-1-032-16883-8 (hbk)
ISBN: 978-1-032-16884-5 (pbk)
ISBN: 978-1-003-25078-4 (ebk)

DOI: 10.4324/9781003250784

Typeset in Melior
by Newgen Publishing UK

Contents

Introduction: We all strive for a strong culture and positive climate — 1

Part 1 Why do leaders need to pay attention to culture and climate? — 3

1 What is culture and why is it important? — 5

2 Extensive domain-specific knowledge is required to create a strong culture and positive climate — 16

3 Setting your school's strategic direction — 24

Part 2 What do leaders need to know about culture and climate? — 35

4 What do high performing teams have in common? — 39

5 The power of expectations — 59

6 Harnessing the drivers of motivation — 71

7 High levels of trust are required to improve outcomes for children — 84

Part 3 How do leaders go about culture change? — 103

8 Influencing culture as a new leader — 107

9 Influencing culture as an established leader — 122

10 Why measuring culture is futile and evaluating it is not much better — 140

Index — 154

Introduction: We all strive for a strong culture and positive climate

In all the schools that you've worked, it is likely that one of them stands out. It'll be the school that was the most enjoyable place to be. Enjoyable because it runs well. Enjoyable because it feels like you're making a difference.

It probably had a strong culture and a positive climate.

Any school leader knows inherently that these conditions are desirable and they all strive to create those conditions. It's tricky though because each school is a beautifully complex organisation with scores of unpredictable human beings, each making sense of their working environment based on their unique prior knowledge. Leaders ought to take this complexity seriously. Doing so requires them to reject simple cause and effect relationships and to recognise the inevitable flaws in their own judgements.

This book is designed around a number of assumptions.

Culture is a persistent problem. It is never fully solved and it is too important for school leaders to take their eye off.

Culture is difficult to define. It incorporates both how a team behaves (including the reasons for and effects of those behaviours) and the effects of them.

Underlying beliefs are important. What the team collectively believes drives their behaviours and has consequences, both positive and negative.

Conversations matter. Beliefs, values and actions spread through regular conversations, particularly with the headteacher.

Culture exists whether leaders design it or not. Leaders ought to deliberately design and carefully maintain how they want their teams to run.

Expert cultural leadership requires extensive knowledge. In order to improve school culture and climate, leaders can become more expert by deliberately building their knowledge.

This book takes the position that becoming more expert in school leadership involves knowing more; knowing more about key educational issues such as curriculum, pedagogy, assessment and behaviour. But also leaders knowing more about their own schools – the specific problems that they're addressing, how exactly they manifest, how colleagues interact with each other and what makes them tick.

This book clarifies the knowledge that leaders require to think carefully about school culture and climate so that they can take informed action to bring about improvement. The reason for writing this book is to support school leaders to build their knowledge of key ideas in cultural leadership. Indeed, the book sets out useful formal knowledge in the various elements of culture and climate and provides plenty of prompts for the reader to inquire into how this manifests in their school.

It is organised into three parts.

Part 1 defines culture and climate, explores the crucial role of leaders' domain-specific knowledge and explains the importance of setting a clear strategic direction.

Part 2 looks in detail at components of culture and climate, including psychological safety, belonging, leaders' expectations, motivation and trust, with plenty of scenarios that exemplify common, specific school situations.

Part 3 details different approaches to how new or established leaders might go about influencing culture and climate. It also explains why leaders shouldn't try to measure or evaluate culture and proposes a different model of inquiry and knowledge building to bring about improvement.

I hope you find it as useful to read as I did to write.

Part I
Why do leaders need to pay attention to culture and climate?

# What is culture and why is it important?

Introduction

School culture makes or breaks leaders' efforts to bring about improvements. When leaders get culture in their schools right, children learn more and colleagues are more motivated. School culture is something that every leader must pay attention to regardless of their unique school context. This chapter explores different ways for school leaders to think of culture and explores its link with climate, proposing that they are two sides of the same coin. It sets the tone for the rest of the book regarding the importance of collective beliefs and assumptions. One of the key themes of the book, knowledge building as a strategy for improvement, is also introduced in this chapter.

> Strong professional environments foster a virtuous cycle in which teachers develop skills faster, stay at a school longer, and improve student learning year over year.
>
> Kraft and Falken[1]

Culture matters

When we spend time in a school, we often get a feeling about the place after even a short time. The interactions that we witness and are part of can often give us a strong idea of whether we'd like to spend longer there or not.

School culture is the collection of behaviours and beliefs shared by colleagues. And it matters. Even though it is the quality of teaching that directly influences outcomes for children, leaders have a significant influence over the conditions in which colleagues work. When leaders get those conditions right, it has been shown to support greater improvement in teacher effectiveness over time than in less favourable conditions[2]. A strong professional environment enables great teaching to happen, but the opposite is equally true. Given that the pursuit of improved outcomes for children is dependent on the culture that leaders establish, arguably the most important aspect of school life for leaders to pay attention to is school culture.

School culture is a persistent problem of school leadership[2]

Whether a school is for infants or teenagers, whether it serves a city centre or a modest village, whether it caters for tens of children or hundreds of children, leaders will need to understand and influence their school culture. This problem is universal because all leaders have to address it.

Framing culture as a problem might seem unpalatable, with some reading this thinking *'Our school culture is not a problem!'*. But the word *problem* needn't have negative undertones. Problem solving is what school leaders do each day. Situations are presented and leaders aim to influence their school systems to make the best of those situations. Some reading this might be thinking *'But we're not reactive, we're proactive!'* Problem solving needn't be thought of as reactive either. Problem solving is leaders understanding their own school context and creating conditions where their children and colleagues flourish. All leaders need to be concerned with this regardless of their context because school context changes.

This is what makes the problem of school culture persistent – it will never be completely solved. Changeable school contexts mean that the status of school culture is always either improving or declining. There may be staffing changes. There may be a shift in strategic priorities. And there may be changes of direction in national policy. No matter what the change, it is certain that it won't be the last and this is why culture will require leaders' attention indefinitely. Fortunately, the problem of school culture is also causal; leaders are able to influence it. Teachers that work in strong professional environments are better and children achieve more[2].

Culture and climate are two sides of the same coin

Often, many words chosen in the discussion of culture are used interchangeably, making understanding the abstract concept particularly difficult for school leaders. What can help is to consider different models that seek to define culture and explain how it works. Two that are particularly helpful, and with clear similarities, are Viviane Robinson's theory of action[3] and Edgar Schein's three levels of culture[4]. In an attempt to provide clarity for school leaders, this book takes the position that there is an important distinction to make between culture and climate even though the two are inextricably linked. Culture is the way that colleagues behave and go about their work (including the reasons why), while climate is the feeling that colleagues have about working in the school. The two do not exist in isolation. Working practices affect how colleagues feel about that work and how they feel contributes to their working practices.

Robinson's *theory of action*

Robinson's theory of action is a useful model to understand how culture and climate are interdependent. It has three components:

- Underlying beliefs, attitude and values
- Behaviours
- Consequences

Robinson suggests that our behaviours are sustained by our beliefs, attitudes and values and that those behaviours lead to consequences, both negative and positive. In Robinson's model, the first two components of beliefs/values and actions can be thought of as culture, while some of the consequences of those actions can be thought of as climate. The dependence of climate on culture is clear in this model, but the inverse relationship is also worth leaders' consideration. How colleagues feel at work can influence their beliefs and again, in turn, their actions, creating a virtuous cycle. Or indeed a toxic one.

In advising leaders on bringing about improvement, Robinson argues that attempting to change others' behaviours only works when the proposed changes align with what they believe and value. If there is tension between the two, then behaviour change is less likely, with reluctant compliance or resistance the only possible outcomes, neither of which are conducive to a productive working environment. Robinson argues that the focus of change should not be on what colleagues *do* but on what they *believe* and *value*. Part 3 of this book considers culture change in detail.

Schein's *three levels of culture*

The importance of beliefs and values in Robinson's model is shared by Schein's model which defines culture at three levels, somewhat similarly to Robinson's theory of action. Schein's distinctions reflect the extent to which culture is visible to those observing it:

- Cultural artifacts
- Espoused beliefs and values
- Underlying assumptions

Cultural artifacts

The most superficial level of Schein's model is termed artifacts. These are the noticeable, collective behaviours, systems and ways of working and, among many others, might include:

- A full car park at 5pm (or an empty one)
- How colleagues dress
- Arriving early (or late) to meetings
- The way that teachers teach
- The way that colleagues interact with each other (for example, relaxed and informal or barely acknowledging each other)

Schein's *artifacts* are relatable to Robinson's *behaviours*, but they also include the results of those collective behaviours – climate. For example:

- The perception of autonomy
- The feeling of being successful
- Motivation
- The feeling of sharing a clear purpose
- Feeling psychologically safe and belonging to the school community
- The level of trust experienced

Where Schein's model is more appropriate for cultural understanding is that culture and climate can be considered under the banner of artifacts. The reason for this is their interdependence. They are entwined to the extent that to separate them would be to oversimplify and underestimate the value of the two concepts.

The cultural artifacts explored in this book include:

- Chapter 4
    - Psychological safety
    - Vulnerability
    - Purpose
- Chapter 5
    - How expectations manifest
- Chapter 6
    - Autonomy
    - Mastery and flow
    - Purpose

- Chapter 7
  - Trust

Artifact: autonomy

Autonomy is a good example of the interdependence of culture and climate. In the case of low autonomy, if colleagues never make decisions for themselves in the tasks they carry out, when they carry them out, how they do them and with whom, this norm becomes noticeable, particularly when colleagues talk about them. Conversations might go along the lines of:

- *Do I need to go and ask if I can do X? I'm not sure and I don't want to get into trouble.*
- *No, it is X that decides that, you need to go and ask.*

The comments and conversations about what is socially permitted (whether explicitly or not) then reinforce collective behaviours and the culture tightens. The actual autonomy exercised by colleagues might be anywhere on a scale from none to complete, but separate to this (and of course closely related), there'll also be colleagues' *perception* of their autonomy. The same level of autonomy afforded by leaders might be perceived differently by different colleagues and it is this perception that influences the climate. Chapter 4 examines autonomy more closely.

Artifact: mastery and flow

Flow is the feeling of satisfaction and enjoyment from a job well done, while mastery is the desire to get better at something that matters. Neither can be experienced without autonomy and all are explored in Chapter 6.

Artifact: purpose

Purpose is the shared knowledge of why colleagues do what they do, which drives the behaviours that the team exhibits. Purpose manifests as climate in the feeling that the team knows why they chose to work in this school and not the school down the road, including what exactly everyone is pulling together to achieve. Chapters 4 and 6 consider the role of purpose in more depth.

Artifact: psychological safety

A feeling of psychological safety is when colleagues feel that they belong to the group and are free from professional threat. Psychological safety, or belonging, contributes to climate, but it is dependent on the interactions between colleagues – the culture that exists in the school. Chapter 4 considers the role of psychological safety and belonging in more detail.

Artifact: trust

Trust is the willingness to be vulnerable based on the deeply held beliefs that our colleagues are competent, reliable and open. Chapter 7 considers the role of trust in more detail.

What colleagues talk about

Cultural artifacts might be noticeable, but paying attention to them as a school leader is only the first step. They alone are only the superficial features of school culture and, to better understand its full complexity, leaders need to know what the team talks about.

The next level of Schein's model is the espoused beliefs and values of the group. These are the things that the individuals in the group say are important. Most schools have some sort of mission, aim or vision statement that seeks to share beliefs and values, but having such a thing does not guarantee it as school culture. The strongest school cultures have alignment between espoused values and artifacts. For example, colleagues might champion the importance of seeing themselves as a team and take deliberate steps to include all colleagues so that the feeling of belonging experienced by all matches what colleagues say.

Problems arise, though, when the espoused values (especially of leaders) do not match the artifacts, for example:

- Putting out token sound bites about reducing workload but doing nothing to address time intensive marking and assessment practices.
- Saying that equality of adult authority in the eyes of children is important yet undermining the authority of those with perceived lower status by swooping in and taking over when behaviour has gone wrong.
- Talking about the importance of trust but perpetuating practices that demonstrate a lack of trust such as asking teachers to hand in planning in advance.
- Describing the curriculum as the progress model but having assessment practices that contradict that very idea.

Underlying assumptions

Espoused beliefs and values can help leaders to understand the cultural artifacts that are noticeable, but it is the third and final layer of Schein's model that contains the most useful information for leaders.

Underlying assumptions are the thoughts and feelings that are taken for granted by the group. They will have been established over time because the group associated those assumptions and beliefs with success that they have experienced. They are the least visible in Schein's model but are the ultimate source of the espoused values and cultural artifacts.

There might be all sorts of underlying assumptions shared by the group, some of them noble, such as:

- We choose to work here because we want to make a difference to this community.
- The least advantaged children in our community deserve the same opportunities as the most advantaged.
- Every child can succeed, given the right support.
- Sharing ideas makes us all better able to improve.

But they could also be less virtuous, such as:

- We turn up, work our hours and nothing more.
- Some children are just not going to succeed.

Some assumptions will be related to the dominant educational philosophy in the school, summarised by Dylan Wiliam[5] as:

- Personal empowerment: allowing children to take greater control of their lives, dealing critically with reality.
- Cultural transmission: passing on the most useful information from one generation to the next.
- Preparation for citizenship: ensuring that children can make informed choices about how they participate in society.
- Preparation for work: to ensure future economic prosperity.

Why assumptions matter

Just like in Robinson's theory of action, it is these underlying assumptions that matter the most in school culture. They dictate how the group behaves and therefore the outcomes achieved by the school, both in terms of what children achieve and what it feels like for colleagues to work there. Because of the importance of underlying assumptions, school leaders need to know what they are, how they spread and how they take hold so that they can influence them.

How beliefs, values and behaviours spread

They spread and are embedded through plenty of interactions between colleagues in various roles. It is through these interactions that the shared knowledge of how the school runs is developed. Leaders will want to influence the interactions that colleagues engage in, which is why talking to everyone, modelling the desired values and using the right language with everyone is so important.

The headteacher is instrumental in these interactions – they set the tone for how others interact because of their status. This status will inevitably bring weight to the beliefs and values promoted by the headteacher, but they do not automatically take root. The group needs to see that the associated practices borne out of those beliefs and values result in success.

Culture and climate exist whether leaders design them or not

Because culture is the shared beliefs and interactions of the group, a culture will become established whether the headteacher designs it or not. The implication for leaders is that, if they do not fully understand and influence the culture they are a part of, the culture will influence them. Understanding and influencing culture is vital to expert school leadership.

One school, different cultures and climates

Leaders might desire a single unifying culture, but, in any school, the conceptual and physical organisation will often mean that different subgroups experience different cultures. The layout of the school influences how colleagues interact and those that come into contact with each other more regularly will often develop their own subculture. The established routes around the school and proximity to amenities such as toilets, photocopier and staff room all influence how colleagues in that area interact.

The conceptual organisation of schools adds another set of subgroups, as those in similar roles interact: teachers, teaching assistants, the administration team, senior leaders, etc. One only has to observe how different subgroups interact to notice their cultural idiosyncrasies, hear what they talk about and infer their underlying assumptions. The larger the school, the more subgroups it will have, and this poses a challenge for school leaders in ensuring that the groups are aligned in their beliefs and assumptions so that what they talk about reinforces the desired culture and climate.

Understanding your school culture and climate: building knowledge

Part 2 of this book takes different elements of culture and climate and provides leaders with prompts to explore the reality of their own school. This chapter has introduced several concepts regarding the definition of culture and climate that leaders ought to be familiar with if they are to understand the complex workings of their schools.

And leaders must understand it in order to be able to bring about improvement. But understanding it is not an easy task. Leaders' own beliefs will likely skew their understanding of the cultural artifacts – certainly a trap to avoid. For example, if leaders see that teachers work through their lunch break without interacting with anyone else, they might deduce that there is a problem between colleagues if their own belief is that lunchtime is for socialising, not working. The reality could well be that workload is a problem and the only way for teachers to leave at a reasonable time and get home to their families is to not stop for a lunch break. The result would be a complete misdiagnosis and possibly a poorly chosen intervention on the leader's part. This could further compound a negative feeling because of the obvious lack of insight shown by the leader.

Another trap for leaders to understand is that the truth does not always rise to the top. Others are far less likely to reveal negative information or demonstrate negative behaviour to leaders and, as such, leaders' opinions can be easily misconceived.

Notice the artifacts

In order for leaders to better understand their own school culture and climate, they might:

- Walk the school and observe the interactions between colleagues. This could include walking the school with different colleagues. What do they notice that the leader has not?
- Spend time in different physical areas of the school (meeting rooms, office, playground, lunch hall, etc.) to notice colleague interactions. Who comes past? Who never does? What do they talk about when they are here?
- Spend time with different groups (year teams, key stage teams, TAs, administration, lunchtime leaders, cover team, etc.) to notice their interactions.
- Accept that their presence will affect others' behaviours and that what they see might not be the actual culture.
- Train other leaders to notice the artifacts – what they notice (or what is revealed to them) will likely be different to the leader's experience.

Listen to the espoused values and beliefs and uncover the underlying beliefs

In order for leaders to better understand their own school culture, they might:

- Ask lots of questions about what colleagues are doing and why.
- Gather the opinions of everyone.
- Accept that, because of their position, others may be reluctant to share the full picture or may tell them what they think they want to hear.
- Have lots of conversations about why they ask colleagues to do what they do and how those intentions are perceived.

Chapter summary

- Colleagues need to flourish if children are to flourish, so leaders need to pay attention to culture.
- Culture is the way that colleagues behave and go about their work, while climate is the feeling that colleagues have about working in their school.
- Colleagues' behaviours are sustained by their beliefs, attitudes, values and underlying assumptions.
- Cultural artifacts are the noticeable, collective behaviours, systems and ways of working that exist in the school.
- Climate includes colleagues' perception of autonomy, the feeling of being successful, motivation, the feeling of a shared purpose, the feeling of psychological safety, the feeling of belonging to the school community and the level of trust they put in others.
- Collective underlying assumptions dictate how the group behaves and therefore the outcomes achieved by the school.
- Culture and climate exist whether leaders deliberately design them or not.
- Leaders need to build their knowledge of the reality of the school's culture and climate in order to bring about improvement.

References

1. Kraft, Matthew A., & Falken, Grace T. (2020) 'Why school climate matters for teachers and students'. *National Association of State Boards of Education.* May 2020. https://nasbe.nyc3.digitaloceanspaces.com/2020/05/Kraft-Falken_May-2020-Standard.pdf
2. Barker, J., & Rees, T. (2020). 'Developing school leadership'. In Lock, S (ed.) *The researchEd guide to school leadership.* Woodbridge: John Catt, pp. 30–31.
3. Robinson, V. (2018). *Reduce change to increase improvement.* Thousand Oaks, CA: Corwin.
4. Schein, E. (1986). *Organizational culture and leadership.* San Francisco, CA: Jossey-Bass.
5. Wiliam, D. (2013). 'Principled curriculum design'. www.tauntonteachingalliance.co.uk/wp-content/uploads/2016/09/Dylan-Wiliam-Principled-curriculum-design.pdf.

Extensive domain-specific knowledge is required to create a strong culture and positive climate

Introduction

Our understanding of great school leadership is shifting. An emerging model of school leadership has at its heart problem solving supported by domain-specific knowledge. A model where leadership expertise is developed through knowledge building to create well-connected mental models that support leaders to take effective action in tackling the persistent problems of school leadership. But domain-specific knowledge can be misunderstood and this chapter explores the different types, providing a framework for subsequent chapters that supports leaders to build important formal knowledge of school improvement as well as the vital hidden knowledge of the culture and climate in their own schools.

An emerging model of school leadership

In the last few decades, the discourse on leadership has been one of traits, styles and generic competencies. While this enabled school leaders to look to other domains for leadership wisdom, it also created a model of school leadership that, somewhat unwittingly, championed the generic. Goleman's leadership styles[1] is one such example, even though that was probably not his intention. Goleman advocated that great leaders know the different styles and select one or a combination appropriate to their situation. This was based on the findings that different styles have different effects on the people being led. Different styles resulted in either positive or negative effects on climate.

In enacting Goleman's model, selecting a style requires sufficient knowledge of whatever is being led, be it a subject or a specific problem that needs to be addressed within a year group or the entire school. The importance of domain-specific knowledge became lost in the discourse on leadership, as leaders and those advising them typically focused on what the leaders *did* and *how they did it* rather than the harder to pin down knowledge that enabled the action.

The previous chapter positioned school culture as a persistent problem of school leadership and that leadership can be thought of as problem solving. However, problem solving isn't a standalone process where leaders apply their problem-solving skills. Nor is it simply the unleashing of leadership traits to get the job done through force of personality.

Problem solving is dependent on what leaders know. When confronted with a problem related to school (and this will be *every* problem that leaders face), it is helpful if leaders have dealt with similar problems before because they will have learned from those experiences. This learning results in leaders building their mental models of different situations over time. Culture and climate will play a vital role in every problem that requires a leader's attention, for example:

- Adopting a new early reading programme
- Implementing changes dictated by national policy
- Improving attainment in maths at the end of key stage 2
- Designing and reviewing the foundation stage curriculum, including systems for teachers to translate that into lessons
- Choosing or refining an assessment system
- Deciding on a marking and feedback policy
- Improving behaviour during unstructured times

All of these are examples of the specifics of problem solving when it comes to school culture. Every school will tackle these things slightly differently and necessarily so because of contextual differences, even between schools that share common contextual features. What leaders know about addressing these problems constitutes their mental model, but mental models are more than simply a collection of facts.

Building your mental models

Mental models are the knowledge that leaders have and how it is organised to enable them to take action. When leaders think about solving problems, they draw upon their mental models to weigh up the problem, consider possible actions they might take and estimate the likely consequences of each. Expert cultural leadership therefore requires a well-connected mental model of educational issues and contextual information[2]. The latter is what Goleman's leadership styles is predicated on – knowing the situation that the school is in and selecting the most appropriate course of action. Effective leaders are cultural architects and, in order to create and maintain a culture where high quality teaching can flourish, there's a body of knowledge that is required to inform leaders' decisions.

In her paper 'Capabilities required for leading improvement'[3], Robinson sets out three capabilities that school leaders must have in order to bring about improvement: (1) Using relevant knowledge from research and experience to (2) solve the complex educational problems that stand in the way of achieving improvement goals while (3) building relationships of trust with those involved. What's great about this definition of leadership is that not a word is wasted. Robinson acknowledges the vital role of domain specific knowledge and recognises different but equally valid sources of knowledge. Robinson sets up knowledge as needing to be used to solve problems, rather than simply having it. The third capability recognises the responsibility to build trust alongside the solving of educational problems, which is examined more closely in Chapter 7.

The term domain-specific knowledge is misunderstood

One of the arguments against the positioning of knowledge as a vital component of school leadership expertise is that there must be more to it than that. Bereiter and Scardamalia reported this back in 1993[4]:

> Most people we talk to do not want to believe that research shows expert performance is mainly a matter of knowledge. They do not necessarily have an alternative explanation ready, but they feel there has to be more to expertise than that.

Some might argue that experience and wisdom, for example, are more important than knowledge. But what are experience and wisdom if they aren't knowledge? Experience is the knowledge gained from doing the job, solving problems and understanding a school's unique context. Knowing what to do when presented with a problem is one way of describing wisdom. Wisdom is based on leaders' knowledge of the problem, how that problem has manifested in the past (either in this school or leaders' previous schools) and how the different choices that leaders have might play out. This is a mental model in its fullest sense. When knowledge is referred to in the discourse on school leadership, it is much more than facts – it encompasses leaders' understanding of the complexity of school culture and climate. The decisions that they make in order to improve them and how well they develop effective professional relationships is dependent on knowledge, both educational and contextual.

This concept of leadership is a welcome alternative to previously dominant models because it provides a clear path for leadership development. Those who aspire to leadership or already hold leadership positions and wish to improve might find it difficult to work on being more affiliative, democratic or setting an appropriate pace (to use the language of Goleman's styles). It is more straightforward for leaders to develop knowledge of educational issues and study the intricacies of their own school context. In order to acquire domain-specific knowledge, it is useful to understand that there are different types.

Formal and hidden knowledge

One way of thinking about the knowledge that leaders need for school improvement is that it can be formal or hidden.

Formal knowledge is easily shared and stated – for example, national curriculum expectations, safeguarding legislation, statutory assessment procedures or evidence-based approaches to curriculum development or pedagogy.

Formal knowledge is necessary for expert cultural leadership but alone is insufficient. Expertise is the combination of formal knowledge with hidden knowledge, of which there are different types.

Hidden knowledge is that which is picked up through previous experiences. Leaders might 'just know' that particular colleagues would be great to lead a particular improvement strategy based on their impressions of them – things they've done before and things they think they are good at or interested in. Leaders may also have a hunch about underlying reasons for a problem (and of course this would need to be investigated).

A part of hidden knowledge is self-regulatory knowledge. Leaders will want to reflect on their previous successes and keep getting better. One important aspect of self-regulatory knowledge is that of one's biases. Leaders will need to ensure that they're aware of their biases in order to actively seek out others to check their hunches and assumptions about what the issues in the school are, along with what is working and what else may work better.

What leaders know determines the culture they establish

If leaders think of culture as the beliefs and values that they advocate, the way they organise their schools and the kinds of things they ask colleagues to do, there is certainly an extensive body of formal knowledge that can help leaders to build their understanding of what appears to have been successful in other settings. It is readily available and includes, among many things, the following:

Learning:

- How memory works
- Cognitive load theory
- Attention
- The difference between learning and performance

Teaching:

- Modelling and explanations
- Checking for understanding
- Feedback
- Managing behaviour
- Regular review
- Scaffolding

There is lots of other formal knowledge tied up in the domains of behaviour, curriculum design and special educational needs, to name just a few. Knowledge of these aspects of education are fundamental to cultural leadership because what leaders know about these things determines what they influence colleagues to do with their time. Consider two scenarios:

Scenario A

A headteacher thinks that, in order for children to remember what they have been taught, they need to regularly review previous material. The headteacher then expects teachers to plan review activities to interrupt children's forgetting and to figure out gaps in what children have understood. Teachers routinely build in review questions and adapt sequences of lessons based on what they notice about children's understanding.

Scenario B

A headteacher thinks that children must be taught the entire curriculum that is planned. The headteacher, through their words and actions, show the importance of curriculum coverage and expects teachers to ensure that all that is planned is taught. Teachers allocate time periods for different units of work, breaking down content into sequences of lessons so that every lesson over the academic year is accounted for. Teachers move through sequences of lessons whether or not children have understood the content because, if they don't, they'll run out of time and some content will not be taught.

In each scenario, the practices are part of what teachers in each school do – the established culture. The culture affects what children learn as well as how teachers feel about working in the school. Leaders' mental models of education translate into school culture and, as such, climate is arguably indirectly dependent on what leaders know. It is therefore leaders' moral imperative to systematically and iteratively build their knowledge of the core business of teaching and learning.

Expertise is more than knowledge

It is not, of course, knowledge alone that adds up to leadership expertise. Robinson's model, described earlier, talks about the *use* of relevant knowledge to solve problems while building trust. Solving problems and building trust are two examples of what might be considered leadership practices, but they are more like rather broad concepts. The latter, building trust, could also be thought of as an outcome and is explored in its own right in Chapter 7.

Leithwood, Harris and Hopkins[5] made seven strong claims about successful school leadership and their second claim wa*s* that almost all successful leaders draw on the same repertoire of basic leadership practices. These basic leadership practices include:

- Setting directions
    - Build a shared vision
    - Identify specific, shared short-term goals
    - Create high performance expectations
    - Communicate the vision and goals

- Building relationships and developing people
    - Stimulate growth in the professional capacities of staff
    - Provide support and demonstrate consideration for individual staff members
    - Model the school's values and practices
    - Build trusting relationships with and among staff, parents and children
    - Establish productive working relationships with colleagues

- Developing the organisation to support desired practices
    - Build a collaborative culture
    - Build productive relationships with families and communities
    - Connect the school to its wider environment
    - Maintain a healthy and safe school environment
    - Allocate resources in support of the school's vision and goals

- Improving the instructional programme
    - Provide instructional support

- Monitor children's learning and school improvement progress
- Buffer staff from distractions to their instructional work

These leadership practices are supported by the elements of culture and climate that are explored in detail in Part 2.

At first glance it may appear that the second practice of building relationships is the most important for culture and climate, but they all will have a significant effect on what colleagues do with their time each day and are therefore all vital to cultural leadership. And, of course, all are dependent on leaders having a great deal of knowledge to address the unique manifestation of the problems in their schools. It is not the practices themselves that create a high performing culture and a great climate – if this were the case then school leadership would be pretty straightforward. Because every school differs contextually, what matters is how leaders apply these practices to their school context and doing so well requires them to have a deep understanding of their own school context.

Becoming more expert: building your knowledge of culture and climate

One of leaders' responsibilities, and the route to greater expertise, is to learn more of the formal knowledge about educational issues that is widely available[2]. This is essential to be able to articulate the educational thinking behind decisions on working practices that form the culture of the school. This reasoning and the articulation of the thinking behind decisions on working practices are key to influencing the team. Cultural buy-in can only be achieved with clear purpose and shared beliefs.

Leaders also have a responsibility to gain greater understanding of the context in which they work. This is acquired through their deliberate day-to-day interactions around the school, noticing, asking questions and following threads. Each chapter in Part 2 provides prompts for how leaders might do this.

- Psychological safety and building belonging (Chapter 4)
- The effect of expectations and bias (Chapter 5)
- The drivers of motivation (Chapter 6)
- Trust (Chapter 7)

Part 3 seeks to provide leaders with important formal knowledge of how culture can be influenced:

- Influencing culture as a new leader (Chapter 8)
- Influencing culture as an existing leader (Chapter 9)

Chapter summary

- The dominant model of leadership from the last few decades emphasised personal traits and generic competencies.

- A different model of leadership is emerging that recognises the importance of domain-specific knowledge.

- Leaders create effective cultures when they have extensive domain-specific knowledge, adapting their practice to respond to their school's unique context.

- Domain-specific knowledge for leading culture includes knowing about educational issues alongside broader concepts such as motivation and trust.

- There are different types of knowledge that leaders should have that contribute to their mental model, both formal educational issues and hidden, relating specifically to the school.

- A leader's domain-specific knowledge and the way it is organised to support action can be thought of as a mental model.

- Becoming more expert at cultural leadership requires leaders to deliberately build their mental model.

References

1. Goleman, D., Boyatzis, R., & Mckee, A. (2013). *Primal leadership.* Boston: Harvard Business Review Press.
2. Barker, J., & Rees, T. (2020). 'Developing school leadership'. In Lock, S (ed.) *The researchEd guide to school leadership.* Woodbridge: John Catt, pp. 32–35.
3. Robinson, V. (2017). 'Capabilities required for leading improvement: Challenges for researchers and developers'. Research conference. https://research.acer.edu.au/cgi/viewcontent.cgi?article=1306&context=research_conference
4. Bereiter, C., & Scardamalia, M. (1993). *Surpassing ourselves.* Chicago: Open Court.
5. Leithwood, K., Harris, A., & Hopkins, D. (2019). 'Seven strong claims about successful school leadership revisited'. *School Leadership & Management*, 40(1), 5–22. DOI: 10.1080/13632434.2019.1596077

3 Setting your school's strategic direction

Introduction

Great school leaders have extensive specialist knowledge in its broadest sense and this enables them to make good decisions about setting the direction of their school. The shared purpose that leaders create in their teams by doing this is a significant contributor to a strong culture and positive climate. This chapter identifies the kinds of things that school leaders must pay attention to in order to tackle the persistent problems of school leadership and how they manifest in their schools. Faced with such a complex task, it is vital for leaders to achieve clarity of thought and this chapter provides a model for thinking clearly about a school's strategic direction.

Show everyone where they're going and make it easy to get there

Chapter 2 described how almost all successful leaders draw on the same repertoire of basic leadership practices and the first of these is setting direction. School leaders' main job is to show everyone where they're going and make it easy to get there. School culture can be the driving force of school improvement if leaders design a future ideal and clearly articulate the practices (and the beliefs that sustain them) that will help to realise that vision. Culture can become the visible and audible manifestation of leaders' expectations. But without a clear strategic direction, there is a risk that the culture that inevitably emerges is one that is neither desirable nor conducive to a great climate or outcomes for children.

Extensive knowledge is required for setting direction

Setting strategic direction requires extensive knowledge about how schools improve and the kinds of things that are worth leaders paying attention to. The ultimate measure of school improvement is that outcomes for children are getting better. But this cannot happen without improvements to the curriculum, teaching or the management of behaviour. And there cannot be systematic improvement of these without a clear understanding of the elements of a great curriculum, what makes great teaching and how children's behaviour might be managed effectively at scale. Leaders must take their extensive knowledge of these things and design professional development and school systems to build shared understanding among colleagues of all those things, supporting them to become more expert as they put those ideas into practice.

When it comes to knowing what to pay attention to, there is research that can help leaders know where to start. Viviane Robinson's work on student-centred leadership[1] identified five leadership practices that have the greatest impact on student outcomes. Establishing goals and expectations had an effect size of 0.42, which shows the importance of clarity of strategic direction and that it most certainly needs to have at its heart a focus on teacher development (effect size of 0.84) to ensure high-quality teaching (effect size 0.42).

These are examples of formal knowledge that all school leaders will need. But all schools differ contextually. Leaders will also need to know their school's strengths and areas for improvement. They need to understand the make-up of the community they serve and what their needs are, and they need to know all about the beliefs and assumptions that their colleagues share, including the extent to which they support or hinder leaders' efforts to bring about improvement. These are all examples of hidden knowledge that are necessary for leaders to use to settle on a strategic direction.

Beware of ambiguity

There is a lot for leaders to know and understand in order to create a compelling direction and this can be further complicated by a lack of clarity in the language that is commonly used when talking about the concept. There are many words with ambiguous meanings that make clarity of thought difficult, including:

- Vision
- Goals
- Strategy
- Aim
- Mission statement
- Outcomes
- Milestones
- Values
- Success criteria

A model for school improvement

A strong culture and climate are dependent on clear direction. Clarity here requires a model to structure leaders' thinking:

Aim	For what purposes does the school exist?
Values	What behaviours make it unique?
Vision	What is the future ideal for how the school runs?
Strategic priorities	What problems do leaders need to solve to realise their vision?
Drivers	What systems will help leaders to address their strategic priorities?
Strategies and their active ingredients	What strategies are required and what are the key concepts and behaviours that need to be implemented for them to be successful?

Start with why – a unifying aim

Every school exists for similar reasons. Dylan Wiliam[2] describes broad reasons for education such as personal empowerment, cultural transmission, preparation for citizenship and preparation for work. This is useful formal knowledge that leaders can use alongside the hidden knowledge of their communities to create a unifying aim around which a desired culture could be built. It is the first signpost that sets the tone for what collective action is trying to achieve. A school's aim should provide an answer to the question: For what purpose does this school exist?

What makes a school unique?

Even though schools exist for broadly the same reasons, parents and colleagues will have different preferences over the school they send their children to or the school they choose to work in. These preferences will be informed by their underlying assumptions and beliefs, as they seek a school culture that aligns with their own values. Leaders need to make it very clear to parents, colleagues and the community what it is that makes their school unique in order to help others to make informed choices.

Culture is the collective actions taken in school and those actions are sustained by what leaders collectively believe and value. If leaders are to influence school culture at all, there needs to be alignment between the existing beliefs and values and the proposed changes that leaders want to make. It is therefore highly beneficial for leaders to determine and, if needed, influence the underlying beliefs and assumptions so that their improvement efforts further down the line might have a better chance of success. The first step in creating this alignment is to be explicit about the values that the community holds. These are the social norms that either already exist or that leaders would like to bring into existence. In establishing school values, there are some things to consider and traps to avoid:

Do	Don't
Ask: • What do we value? • What is our identity? • What are our deep-rooted beliefs?	
Collaborate with colleagues, parents, children and those responsible for governance	Impose the values of an unrepresentative group on the whole community
Limit the number of values to ensure they are memorable	Have a long list of values that are difficult to remember
Phrase them as verbs to enable action	Phrase them as abstract nouns
Define them and use stories to exemplify them	Assume that everyone knows their meaning
Make a communication plan to ensure they are known and lived by all	Assume that everyone will remember them all the time
Use them to guide decision-making	Let them become simply words on the wall

Schools having values is rather common, but the way they are organised and phrased can sometimes limit their effectiveness. A common mistake is having too many, which renders them forgettable. Another is to phrase them as abstract nouns rather than verbs. It is far easier to act on the value 'be honest' than it is to act on the value of 'integrity', for example.

Stories are psychologically privileged and so using them to define values once they have been defined makes it easier to communicate them widely and for them to be understood and remembered. A school's values should provide the answer to the question: What makes colleagues choose to work here rather than the school down the road?

What do you need to pay attention to in order to improve?

Leaders will have an idea of what they need to work on to improve their school, based on rigorous self-evaluation. Choosing the right response is altogether more complex. Consider the issue of poor school performance in maths at the end of

KS2. Raising attainment in maths would be the priority, but how? There might be all sorts of contributing factors to the poor attainment:

- Low-level disruption in lessons
- Lack of engagement from children
- Children's lack of knowledge and fluency of foundations – facts and calculation procedures
- Teachers' explanations, scaffolding and use of formative assessment
- Curriculum sequencing

From these possible factors, leaders might choose to prioritise one or a combination of behaviour, pedagogy or curriculum development. Each would require close attention to the actions that colleagues take each day when teaching maths.

Further diagnoses of this and other issues may yet yield further priorities and then there is the risk of having too many. If everything is a priority, then nothing is. The difficulty is choosing a small number of priorities and doing them well. The impact of making the right choice here is significant. A clear purpose, as will be explored in Chapters 4 and 6, is vital for colleagues to feel motivated. Choosing a manageable number of priorities and guiding attention to them at different times will dictate workload patterns and, in turn, climate. A school's strategic priorities should provide the answer to the question: What do leaders need to pay attention to in order to improve?

> **Example**
>
> Mary and her leadership team consider the persistent problems of school leadership and use them as a framework to determine the school's priorities. She poses the question: What do leaders need to pay attention to in order to improve? Ideas are refined and tested out with colleagues and they finally settle on four priorities:
>
> - A calm and purposeful environment
> - Growing our own
> - A curriculum to remember
> - A strong start
>
> The leadership team choose the wording very carefully to make the priorities memorable. 'A calm and purposeful environment' reflects their priority of maintaining the good behaviour of the vast majority of children and seeking to improve it for a minority of children in terms of their engagement with learning. 'Growing our own' reflects their

> priority of providing great professional development opportunities for all, as well as creating succession plans for key leadership positions. 'A curriculum to remember' reflects their priority of curriculum development, including design that supports children to understand and remember all that they have been taught. 'A strong start' reflects their priority of excellent early years practice as well as improving transitions between year groups and key stages.

Describe the future

Vision is a detailed description of the future – what leaders, in consultation with their colleagues and communities, wish the school to be like. A compelling vision is important because it provides concrete examples of what everyone will be trying to achieve. A vision that details working practices and how those in the community treat each other brings expectations to life and the destination that is described helps leaders to focus their improvement efforts. A vision works well when it is related to the school's strategic priorities.

> **Example**
>
> Mary and her team spend time pooling ideas about what the future ideal might look like in their four strategic priorities, discussing ideas with other colleagues and refining them.
>
> **A calm and purposeful environment**
>
> Children are happy and feel as if they belong to their friendship group, their class, their school and their community. All relationships at school are rooted in kindness, inclusion and gratitude. Children enjoy feeling successful and have the confidence to make mistakes. They see the value in learning so they work hard. Children take up varied responsibilities and leadership positions, which encourages pride in their school and their community.
>
> **Growing our own**
>
> Varied continuous professional development opportunities ensure colleagues gain expertise. We provide opportunities for career progression to keep our talented colleagues in our community. Succession planning protects the future of our schools and we contribute to system leadership through school-to-school support.
>
> **A curriculum to remember**
>
> The curriculum is coherently planned, sequenced and well taught so children are able to learn. Rich experiences in and outside the classroom, beyond school and in the wider community help them to make sense of the world. Children have good emotional, mental and physical health. Diversity and equality are celebrated and promoted

> throughout our curriculum and in community events. Oracy and communication are prioritised throughout our curriculum to give children the tools they need for the next stage of their education.
>
> **A strong start**
>
> Even before children start at our schools, our interactions with joining families show them that they belong to our community. Clear and timely communication means that children are fully prepared for their first days. Transition between year groups and key stages involves multiple advance visits to new classrooms and shared areas to ensure familiarity with adults and surroundings. When new colleagues join our schools, they receive personalised induction support to feel successful.

Strategies and their active ingredients

Culture will play an important role in whatever strategic priorities school leaders choose because addressing priorities requires collective action. This might include colleagues doing something new, it might involve colleagues doing something that they already do better or it might involve colleagues stopping doing something that has a low impact for the time it takes. Leaders also need to bear in mind that changes to what they want colleagues to do must align with collective beliefs and assumptions and that influencing these strategically is a significant part of school improvement.

Each strategic priority will be addressed by strategies that leaders select and develop. Each strategy will contribute significantly to the culture because they will draw attention to the actions that need to be taken to address the priorities and realise the vision. Below are examples of the kind of explicit strategies leaders might need in order to address common priorities:

- Behaviour strategy
- Teaching strategy
- Assessment strategy
- Curriculum strategy
- Reading strategy
- Writing strategy
- Maths strategy

- SEND strategy
- Pupil premium strategy
- CPD strategy

Where these strategies directly influence culture is through specifying the behaviours and concepts that are required – termed 'active ingredients':

> It is easier to implement an intervention if it is clear which features need to be adopted closely to get the intended outcomes. These features are sometimes called the 'active ingredients' of the intervention. A well specified set of 'active ingredients' captures the essential principles and practices that underpin the approach. They are the key behaviours and content that make it work.
>
> *Education Endowment Foundation*[3]

Example

Mary and her leadership team have chosen a calm and purposeful environment as a strategic priority and Mary knows that a clear behaviour strategy is needed to realise the vision that they have described. Through wide reading, drawing on experiences, discussion with colleagues and visits to other schools, the leadership team settle on a set of active ingredients for their behaviour strategy that their practices will be built on:

- Consistent, calm adult behaviour
- First attention to the best conduct
- Equality of adult authority
- Reasonable adjustments
- Analyse, don't personalise
- Positive language choice
- Relentless routines, taught and practised
- Enable success because success breeds motivation

Mary and her team build the expectations of colleagues, training and systems around these concepts and behaviours.

Understanding your school culture and climate: building knowledge of self

Achieving a desired culture and climate is dependent on understanding the culture that already exists, but this starts with leaders understanding their school's strategic direction:

- What is the school's aim? Why does it exist?
- What are the school's values? What sets it apart from other schools?
- What are the school improvement priorities? To what extent are they manageable?
- What strategies have leaders chosen to address these priorities? What are the active ingredients of those strategies?

Having reflected on these questions, leaders will have summarised the strategic direction of their school. They may have recognised one of several scenarios:

1. They answered the prompts comfortably

If they were able to do so, it is likely that they have a strong idea of the strategic direction they want for their school. They may not use the same language as in the prompts. However, just because it is well defined does not mean it is the lived experience of all colleagues.

2. They answered the prompts partially

It may be that they were able to answer some of the prompts. This might not be because they have not been thought through; it might be that they have fallen by the wayside. Equally, it might very well be that they have not been thought through enough.

3. They were not able to answer the prompts

Again, this does not necessarily mean that these things do not exist – they may have been under communicated. However, it may well be that they do not exist.

Understanding your school culture and climate: building knowledge of others

Using only their own reflection is insufficient to gather a rounded understanding and leaders need to seek out others' perceptions in order to be in a position to influence them.

- What is the school's aim? Why does it exist?
- What are the school's values? What sets them apart from other schools?
- What are the school improvement priorities? To what extent are they manageable?
- What strategies have been chosen to address these priorities? What are the active ingredients of those strategies?

Designing the culture you want

It is important for leaders to have an idea of their desired strategic direction. In order to think this through, the same questions are useful:

- What would I choose as the school's aim? Why does it exist?
- What would I choose as the school's values? What sets it apart from other schools?
- What would I choose as the school improvement priorities?
- What strategies would I choose to address these priorities? What would I advocate as the active ingredients of those strategies?

Chapter summary

- Clear strategic direction is a prerequisite for a great school culture.
- Having a model for strategic direction can help leaders to bring structure to their thinking about the culture they wish to create.
- Engaging everyone in the process of clarifying a shared strategic direction is vital for buy-in.
- An aim is an overarching phrase that drives the school's activities.
- Values are the North Star for how the community should behave.
- Values are what make a school unique.
- A vision is what leaders want the school to be like in the future – a direction to travel in.
- Strategic priorities are chosen to help realise the aim based on where the school is now.
- School culture is driven by the aim, values and strategic priorities.

- Each priority is backed up by a number of strategies.
- Strategies detail the behaviours required to bring about improvement.
- These behaviours are the nuts and bolts of the culture that leaders seek to create.

References

1. Robinson, V. (2011). Student-centered leadership. San Francisco, CA: Jossey-Bass.
2. Wiliam, D. (2013). 'Principled curriculum design'. www.tauntonteachingalliance.co.uk/wp-content/uploads/2016/09/Dylan-Wiliam-Principled-curriculum-design.pdf.
3. Education Endowment Foundation. (2019). *Putting evidence to work: A School's guide to implementation.* https://educationendowmentfoundation.org.uk/education-evidence/guidance-reports/implementation.

Part 2
What do leaders need to know about culture and climate?

Part 2 preamble

What does it take for school leaders to learn about culture and climate from other domains?

Introduction

Examples of great leadership are all around us, both within and outside the domain of education. There are plenty of lessons to be learned about creating a strong culture and a positive climate from education research and from research beyond education. This preamble sets the tone for Part 2 of the book, identifying the key elements of culture and climate.

Learning from other domains is appealing

The dominant leadership narrative of previous decades, that of the importance of leadership traits or skills, has led to a whole genre of leadership advice and wisdom on bookshelves, in blogs and in podcasts. Higher-profile, more universally understood and experienced domains such as sport and business capture our attention and the opportunity to learn from those who have had incredible success or who we look up to is alluring.

Generic leadership advice on developing culture and climate needs to be combined with educational domain-specific knowledge

But this leadership narrative has developed from the specificity of those domains, where leaders solve their own domain-specific problems. The culture in a sports team is geared towards winning competitions. The culture in a business is geared towards making profit. Both of these are entirely different problems that need to be solved compared to the endeavours of school leaders. The persistent problems of school leadership are first and foremost about the core business of teaching, including the design of a coherent curriculum, making sure that it is well taught and that children actually learn it. School leaders cannot simply transplant another organisation's solutions to their educational problems when those problems are not the same.

All domains have people in common

When it comes to learning from other domains, though, there is perhaps an opportunity to learn about some of the persistent problems of school leadership, namely those of culture, administration and self. Why? Because it is reasonable to suggest that these are not just persistent problems of school leadership but of organisational leadership. While the problems may manifest slightly differently, they do have people in common. People who arguably need the same conducive environment to be happy, productive and motivated in their chosen line of work.

Beware the superficial features of other domains

In seeking leadership advice or wisdom from outside of education, leaders will have to look for the generic, which is, after all, the focus of many leadership books written and marketed to appeal to a wide audience. Some of this will be useful – nuggets applicable to them as education leaders – if they simply think about the extent to which it might support their endeavours in schools. In thinking this through, leaders must attempt to distil the fundamental concepts and processes that are described as contributing to success in other realms, being careful not to pay attention merely to the surface features, and always seeking to combine this knowledge with their formal knowledge of education and the hidden knowledge of their own school context.

Lessons in cultural leadership from education and beyond

Part 2 of this book is made up of four chapters.

Chapter 4 looks at applying research into high-performing teams in a wide number of different domains to the domain of education. It exemplifies how school leaders can design their culture and affect their school climate using the key ideas of building psychological safety, sharing vulnerability and establishing purpose.

Chapter 5 takes a study of the effects of expectations on student performance and explores the possibility of leaders' expectations of colleagues improving their performance. It exemplifies how school leaders might notice and adjust the non-verbal communications of their expectations of colleagues to support them to perform at a higher standard.

Chapter 6 looks at applying research into motivation from the corporate domain to the domain of education, exemplifying how school leaders can design a culture that motivates using the key ideas of autonomy, mastery and purpose.

Chapter 7 explores the application of research into trust from various sources, drawing together common elements most relevant to school leadership.

Develop your leaders' cultural leadership expertise, chapter by chapter

The chapters that follow are structured in a way that supports readers to develop their expertise in cultural leadership. Each chapter begins with explanations of interesting research from different domains and considers its application to school leadership. Each chapter includes prompts for readers to use to understand more about how these concepts manifest in their schools before ending with suggestions about what leaders might do with the information gathered.

What do high performing teams have in common?

Introduction

The highest performing teams in different domains all around the world have three things in common: they build safety, they share vulnerability, and they establish purpose. Psychological safety is a prerequisite for high performance and, indeed, leaders aiming to bring about cultural change will find their efforts futile without the team feeling psychologically safe. This chapter looks in detail at the specific behaviours involved and explores their use in a school context. Each behaviour is exemplified in a wide range of leadership scenarios and leaders are provided with prompts to develop their hidden knowledge of their own school.

Build safety, share vulnerability and establish purpose

Daniel Coyle studied the highest performing teams across the world in different domains[1] and shared their features. These included teams from the world of sport, the military, the film industry and more, and Coyle found that what they had in common was that they:

- build safety,
- share vulnerability and
- establish purpose.

Teams flourish when colleagues feel psychologically safe

In schools, the extent to which colleagues feel that they belong to the team, the local community and the education community can have an influence on their motivation and commitment, and this makes a difference to the school climate.

DOI: 10.4324/9781003250784-7

How the team feels may seem disconnected to achieving the desired outcomes for children, but a positive climate is a prerequisite for those outcomes and, as such, it is something for leaders to pay attention to.

So, what does building safety look like? What behaviours need to be modelled and encouraged amongst the team? Knowing these things can help leaders deliberately craft a high performing culture.

Some belonging cues need no educational context

Some of the belonging cues that Coyle identified in the highest performing teams need no educational context:

- Show warmth and kindness in every interaction
- Give good eye contact
- Engage in frequent, energetic exchanges
- Close physical proximity (but not too close)
- Prevent interruptions
- Eat together
- Encourage humour and laughter
- Treat individuals as unique and valued
- Give small attentive courtesies
- Show that you care

These behaviours are superficial; any of us is capable of doing these things, but our personalities mean that we sit on a particular point on a continuum for each individually. It might be tempting to look at this list and think that we either do them naturally or we do not. This book takes the position that all behaviours can be learned and we can all improve given timely feedback and deliberate attention. These behaviours are grouped together because they can be learned and enacted without the need for educational expertise. They may be generic but they are important. Important not in isolation, but in getting on with the work of school leadership. Take, for example, showing warmth and kindness. It is relatively easy to do this in a social situation where there is no work pressure. Leaders can sometimes feel frustration under the pressures of leading a school and one of the first things out of the metaphorical window might be warmth and kindness.

> **Example**
>
> Bea is a senior leader in a fairly large primary school. She knows most of her colleagues very well, having worked there for a number of years, but she is aware that there are some colleagues she doesn't know well at all and has had fewer interactions with. While she has strong bonds with many colleagues, interactions with a lunchtime controller (Shazia) are, at the most, simply pleasant and polite. Bea wonders whether Shazia's working pattern means she does not feel as if she belongs as much as other colleagues. Bea decides to do more to build relationships between Shazia and other colleagues. She starts making a deliberate effort to welcome Shazia when she arrives each day, getting to know her as they walk together to the lunch hall. After a few days, Bea knows about some of her interests and the names of her children, who go to a nearby school. As they are walking to the hall, a teaching assistant (Belinda) walks by and Bea knows that her daughter goes to the same school as one of Shazia's daughters. Bea leaves them to it and Susan and Belinda chat for a few minutes about their children.

Belonging cues bound up in education

However, these belonging cues were not the entirety of what Coyle observed as ways of encouraging psychological safety. While the behaviours on the previous list are generic, the fact that leaders need to build belonging *alongside* running their subject, phase or school cannot be overlooked. In seeking to build psychological safety using the following ideas from Coyle's observations, school leaders will need to draw on their formal knowledge of educational issues as well as their hidden knowledge of their own school context, their colleagues and themselves:

- Make mixing happen
- Ask questions to draw others out
- Celebrate the humblest of tasks
- Narrate others' role in the future
- Create connections between people

Make mixing happen

Sometimes, schools settle into routines and patterns regarding with whom colleagues come into contact. In some larger schools, colleagues in different year groups might sometimes go days without seeing each other or even longer without interacting meaningfully. Making mixing happen involves understanding the reasons why mixing might not be happening and creating opportunities throughout the school day to interact in a way that not only builds belonging but also supports colleagues to be better at their jobs. The structure of the school day is one consideration. If there are staggered break times for children of different ages, colleagues from one phase won't see others from another phase during that break. In many cases, staggered break times are unavoidable due to space, but leaders' decisions on things like this need to consider the impact on socialising and collaboration.

Another consideration is the layout of the school. If the staff room is at one end of the school, it may be that logistics deter some from going there. Maybe there is not enough time to drop children at the playground from break, go to the toilet, grab a drink, etc. before needing to head back. A more central staff room, if possible, could make mixing easier in this instance.

Then there is room layout. The staff room is likely to be the one room that sees the most interaction, so making the most of the space and choosing a layout carefully is important. Perhaps seats are around the outside of the room, all facing in. When the staff room is being used, this could contribute to interesting, whole group conversations but, equally, it might inhibit them. Maybe smaller groups of furniture might be better suited to the colleagues in the school who prefer it that way.

These examples are social, but leaders also need to consider making mixing happen in the context of CPD and improving the school. Teaching can be a lonely job – adults spend most of their time in the classroom in which they work. Leaders can make mixing happen by establishing the norm of visiting other classrooms. Cover might be tricky, but, even if it is for a short period of time, the mixing can trigger conversations and further interaction. But leaders need to plan for this. Directing people to certain classrooms or other colleagues to see a particular practice or prompting others to ask a colleague about a particular issue are both examples of encouraging mixing.

> **Example**
>
> Micky is the maths leader and has been working hard to embed the use of concrete manipulatives across the school. He knows, through conversations and from walking around the school during maths lessons, that one teacher (Kat) routinely uses them and another (Simran) uses them only sporadically. He knows that neither is necessarily good or bad, that what matters is whether children understand what they are being taught, and he is keen to get people talking to each other to understand this more. He notices that both are teaching column subtraction and asks them to get together briefly after school. 'Thanks for making the time to meet. As you know, we've been talking about the use of concrete manipulatives recently and I noticed that you both went about teaching column subtraction differently. Remember, what is important is not the manipulatives themselves but whether children are learning. Simran, how did you go about it?' Simran explains that she used base ten blocks. 'Kat, what about you?' Kat explains that she tried using base ten blocks but it slowed some children down who already had a fairly good idea of what to do. Simran agrees. She has noticed this but thought she had to have some

> manipulatives out in every lesson. Micky lets Kat expand on her experience, explaining that they are there for some children to use if necessary. When Micky concludes the meeting, Kat and Simran stay to chat more about maths.

Ask questions to draw others out

This can be exemplified in the everyday problem solving that leaders engage in. Nothing shows how much you are valued more than being asked your opinion on something important.

> **Example**
>
> Richard, the deputy headteacher, thinks that the way lunchtimes are run (getting children into the hall with their lunch and seated) needs refining. Richard knows that this is just his assumption, so he seeks out the opinions of the lunchtime controllers. They agree that how children are called, where they line up and the doors they use seems inefficient. Richard has an idea about what could be better, but he knows how important it is to gather the opinions of others to help them to feel part of the team. 'How would you get children into the hall?' asks Richard. They discuss different ideas and what the consequences might be before settling on a plan to trial next week.

What matters is the follow through. If colleagues give leaders feedback that a system isn't working and make a suggestion, it is well worth trialling. If the responses are not acted on, leaders cannot be surprised if they stop coming at all.

Celebrate the humblest of tasks

One way of looking at this is to recognise the people that do the humblest tasks. Sometimes in schools, teachers can find themselves at the top of an unintended hierarchy over teaching assistants and administration or site staff. Leaders' work can sometimes be centred around the work that teachers do alone, including CPD, efforts to ensure work/life balance and simply the amount of time spent talking to teachers compared to other colleagues. If leaders celebrate the humblest of tasks through regular narration to colleagues, children and parents, that can further show that everyone matters and belongs.

Another way of looking at this is to make the humblest of tasks things that everyone does. The New Zealand rugby team, the All Blacks, are notable for the longevity of their success, and James Kerr wrote a book about how they have achieved this[2]. The first is named *sweep the sheds*. It refers to the expectation that everyone does this job, that we should never be too big to do the small things that need to be done. This is a wonderful mindset to be modelling for children and deserves a high-profile place in a school's cultural artifacts. There are multiple tasks that fit this profile throughout the school day, such as picking up litter, stacking chairs, tidying shared areas or emptying the dishwasher, but what does it look like for school leaders? Is it important for school leaders to do this? Absolutely, but there is more to it than simply doing. It's about involving others.

- Don't walk past someone doing such a job without helping
- Draw in others when you're doing such a job to encourage team responsibility
- Narrate the importance of the little things at incidental moments
- Ask for help to carry out these tasks

These tasks might take time away from the important work of school improvement, but they set the tone for a cohesive culture, on which school improvement is dependent.

Narrate others' role in the future

When colleagues know that they have a role in the future of the school, it can contribute to a feeling of belonging and safety. For this to have any authenticity, leaders need to be able to narrate *what* the future looks like, something that requires a great deal of educational knowledge (and is described in detail in Chapter 3). This is not only formal knowledge of the educational vision but also informal knowledge – of colleagues' strengths, areas for improvement, career aspirations and relationships with others.

> **Example**
>
> Noeman is the key stage 1 leader and in his team is a teaching assistant (Clare) who is studying for a degree with the aim of enrolling in teacher training and qualifying as a teacher. 'Clare, it will be great to have you teaching a class here in key stage 1 when you qualify. You know the children and the families so well and having you as their teacher will be fantastic. On another note, we're reviewing our history curriculum soon and I know how much you love history. It would be great to talk to you about your ideas for our key stage 1 history curriculum. Then you can teach it with me!'

Create connections between people

Being able to connect others relies on extensive knowledge of what they have in common or interests they share. It would be lovely to create connections on a personal level, but this alone probably won't result in improved educational provision. An alternative is for leaders to create educational connections and, to do this, leaders need to know things such as:

- What each colleague is good at
- What each colleague wants or needs to get better at
- What specialist knowledge each colleague has
- The extent to which a particular colleague has capacity for such conversations
- With whom each colleague tends to mix or not mix already

This informal knowledge would mean that decisions about making mixing happen are rooted in educational improvement.

> **Example**
>
> Yasmin is the reading leader and has worked hard to establish a system of how reading is taught across the school. A new teacher (James) joined the school mid-year in year 5 and is very keen to improve the provision for the weakest readers. James has picked up that, although the weakest readers in year 5 have good phonological awareness, their reading fluency is poor, so he asks Yasmin for advice. Yasmin is more than capable of giving sound advice, but she knows that a teacher in year 2 (Mel) has great expertise in helping children to improve fluency. Yasmin arranges for her and James to watch Mel teaching reading so that she can narrate some of the things that Mel does. After the lesson, Yasmin encourages James to talk more to Mel about what she did and what she believes to be a good way to approach the problem of reading fluency in year 5.

Good leaders are vulnerable

Good leaders accept that they do not know everything and are not threatened by the insecurity of admitting ignorance. The concept of vulnerability is explored in more detail in the context of trust in Chapter 7, but, in the meantime, Coyle identifies the following ways that leaders might share vulnerability:

- Seek feedback
- Face uncomfortable truths head on
- Debrief decision-making

Seek feedback

Precisely because of being in a position of leadership, leaders probably will not see or hear the reality of school life from others' perspectives. It is common for others to tell leaders what they think they want to hear or show them what they think they want to see. However, leaders still need to seek accurate feedback about the school and about their leadership.

> **Example**
>
> Hassan is the headteacher of a small school. He recognises that, in smaller schools with fewer colleagues to take on various roles, everyone has a number of responsibilities and workload can be an issue. Hassan knows that he needs to minimise workload as much as possible while making sure that the school provides a great education for children. He takes the time to meet with each colleague in turn with the intention of finding out what he can do better to balance these competing pressures. He asks three questions:
>
> - What is one thing I do that you'd like me to continue doing?
> - What is one thing I do not do frequently enough that you'd like me to do more often?
> - What can I do to enable you to be more effective?

The important thing is to act on the feedback. It can be difficult for leaders to hear negative feedback on practices they have invested in and they all need to be aware of the sunk cost fallacy – persisting with an initiative because of time invested in it despite it appearing not to add value. Constructive feedback will not continue to be shared if previous feedback is not heard or taken seriously.

Face uncomfortable situations head on

It can be tempting to avoid uncomfortable situations. Often in schools, this might take the form of addressing instances when standards are not being met and children are being negatively affected. Viviane Robinson champions the idea of *open to learning conversations*[3], where leaders deliberately present their views as a hypothesis to be tested rather than absolute fact.

This process enables leaders to develop trusting relationships while addressing difficult issues. Sometimes, leaders might ask leading questions, hoping to come across as affiliative and, at the same time, hoping that the person in front of them will bring up the issue that needs to be discussed. Robinson suggests guiding values for open to learning conversations:

- Increase the validity of information (which includes thoughts, opinions, reasoning, references and feelings)

- Increase respect (treating others as well intentioned, interested in learning and capable of contributing to our own)

- Increase commitment (creating ownership of decisions through transparent and shared processes)

The important aspect of this work on sharing vulnerability is to be upfront about concerns but to position these concerns as something to be explored rather than assuming them to be valid.

> **Example**
>
> Bushra is the assistant headteacher and also the SENDCo. It is the time of year to review targets on SEND support plans and set new ones where necessary. One teacher (Beth) didn't meet the deadline and when she did send them to Bushra, they fell below the standard that Bushra expected and she is worried that children with SEND are not getting the right support in that class.
>
> Bushra: 'Beth, I need to tell you about a possible concern I have about how children with SEND are supported in your class. I looked at the SEND support plans you sent me and they seem to have been rushed. They are not up to your usual high standard – would this be fair to say?'
>
> Beth looks a little taken aback and explains how busy she has been recently. Her work as an ECT mentor has been challenging as she adjusts to a new system and she has been planning for the Nativity performance too.
>
> Bushra: 'What I'm hearing is that you're juggling a lot of responsibilities. Is that right?'
>
> Beth agrees and adds more. She explains that the paperwork required is onerous and that the time taken to complete the paperwork could be better spent on more important things.
>
> Bushra: 'What leads you to believe that SEND support plans are less important than other things?'
>
> Beth clarifies that she thinks supporting children is important. She goes on to explain how she has been supporting children with SEND in her class and Bushra realises that Beth has a much stronger idea of what is needed than is evident on the plans she sent. Beth shows Bushra some of the work that the children have produced.
>
> Bushra: 'Well, I think we can both agree that what you're doing for those children sounds great. It is so nice to hear how much thought has gone into what you do for

> them. I think the problem is mine – what doesn't work about completing SEND support plans?'
>
> Beth explains that the formatting is terrible. Sometimes, typing into boxes makes everything else move and then it takes forever to make it look acceptable. She also explains that there is so much duplication of information required that it is really frustrating.
>
> Bushra: 'It sounds as if I have some work to do to make the process easier. There are things that have to be on these documents, but I'd love your input on how we can make them easier for teachers to complete'.

Debrief decision-making

Debriefing decisions that have been made to build a shared mental model for future decisions is a vital routine for leaders to establish. Leaders make a huge number of decisions each day and that decision-making is based on what they know. For example, leaders may decide to shuffle teaching assistants around because of a resignation. Once the decision has been made, the reshuffle has happened and the dust has settled, it would be worth returning to the decision to reflect on how it was managed for two reasons. The first is that there may still be some niggles that need working out – often, requiring colleagues to change what they do can have a negative effect on their morale or the interactions they have with others. The second is that this is a situation that will almost certainly pop up again and therefore knowing in what ways the decision-making and execution of the plan worked and in which ways it did not will allow leaders to make better decisions next time.

Sometimes, leaders might need to make decisions with insufficient knowledge, such as when the government closed schools to most children during the coronavirus pandemic. Leaders can develop their expertise by taking the time to talk through decisions that have been made. A vital component of this is leaders' willingness to accept that they may not have made the right decision and to explore other possible courses of action with colleagues.

A useful set of questions for debriefing decision-making is:

- What did we know at the time?

- What would it have been useful to know at the time?

- What options did we have?

- Did we explore other options fully?

- How well did we communicate our decision?

- How well did we follow our decision through?
- What would we do if presented with a similar situation again?

Narrate a clear purpose

Chapter 3 described the effect that having a clear strategic direction has on culture and climate. Having this clarity makes it easier to enact the strategies that Coyle identifies as establishing purpose:

- Overcommunicate vision, values and strategic priorities
- Narrate a link between the present and a future ideal
- Establish vivid, memorable rules of thumb
- Distinguish between where proficiency is needed and where creativity is needed
- Read energy signals and boost when a lull might occur

Overcommunicate vision, values and strategic priorities

Taking regular opportunities to get everyone thinking about what leaders are trying to achieve and what makes them unique is an important part of establishing purpose. These moments are for calibration, to keep collective action focused on what matters. Coyle found that naming and ranking priorities was a useful way to do this. A senior leadership team might do this at regular intervals throughout the year to help everyone know what to focus on and what can take a back seat. Making a communication plan is a useful process to go through to ensure a regular and meaningful sharing of vision, values and priorities. The plan would need to consider the different audiences and should include:

- Colleagues
- Children
- Parents
- Those responsible for governance
- The wider community
- Prospective parents
- Prospective new recruits

There will also be a number of vehicles for communicating the information, including:

- Incidental conversations around the school
- Staff meetings
- Assemblies
- Parent newsletters and other communications
- Social media posts
- Reports to those responsible for governance
- The school website
- The school prospectus
- Parent tours and open evenings

Deliberately planning the messages that go to each group in the community is a good way to ensure that the message received is clear about what the school stands for.

Narrate a link between the present and a future ideal

Coyle also described how the highest performing teams harness the power of story. Describing the future and the path to it provides another interaction with the purpose. Coyle advocates *filling the windscreen with stories*. Such stories include successes and how they have been achieved that draw attention to the behaviours that leaders wish to see – the enactment of the strategic priorities.

> **Example**
>
> Biya is the headteacher of a large school and wants to promote a collaborative culture between teachers where they share planning effectively and support one another to keep workload low and teaching quality high. Biya explains what she wants to see and makes sure that school systems are set up to enable this, such as easy file sharing and protected time together. To keep momentum, though, Biya knows that she needs to draw attention to where it is happening and the successes. She and her leadership team look out for it happening and then share stories of it. Widely. 'It was great to see the team collaborate on history curriculum planning last week. The ideas were far more historically valid and the sequence of lessons far more coherent than if any one individual were to do this themselves. And they've saved hours of time! Great job! Imagine the difference we can make when these conversations are happening for every subject in every year group...'

Establish vivid, memorable rules of thumb

There are many predictable situations in schools that leaders can formulate desirable responses to. Doing so can free up time and energy to focus on implementing ideas well while reinforcing purpose and priorities. The following examples are of what teachers might do if children are exhibiting particular needs in reading, writing and maths:

Reading

If a child struggles with attention and effort	<ul><li>Ensure a feeling of success</li><li>Consistent reading routines</li><li>Narrate reading as the class norm</li><li>Ensure a feeling of belonging to a group that reads</li><li>Individual attention about book choice/reading at home</li></ul>
If a child has poor phonological awareness	<ul><li>Explicit phonics instruction</li><li>Practice of phoneme manipulation</li></ul>
If a child has poor reading speed/fluency	<ul><li>Reading to an adult to support teaching through correction</li><li>Repeated oral reading</li><li>Ensure adults do not interrupt attempts to decode</li><li>No reliance on sustained silent reading</li><li>Explicit spelling instruction</li><li>Regular exposure to high frequency words</li><li>Assisted reading with the adult gradually becoming less dominant</li></ul>
If a child has poor language comprehension	<ul><li>More and higher quality interaction with taught vocabulary</li><li>More engaging with an adult reading aloud to them</li><li>Increase use of quality non-fiction texts</li></ul>

Writing

Grammatical inaccuracy	<ul><li>Adults to reframe sentences for children to mimic orally</li><li>Additional practice in rehearsing a model text</li><li>Sentence level practice of accuracy and punctuation</li><li>Tailored review questions for each lesson</li></ul>	Fewer opportunities to write, insisting on higher quality to avoid reinforcing misconceptions
Poor spelling	<ul><li>Explicit spelling instruction</li><li>Tailored review questions for each lesson</li><li>Which is the tricky bit?</li></ul>	

Laboured handwriting	• Check pencil grip/posture • Letter formation instruction • Prioritise fluent formation and joining before neatness • Highlighter guides	
Low motivation/effort	• Ensure a feeling of success • Consistent writing routines • Narrate writing as the class norm • Ensure a feeling of belonging to the group that does writing	

Maths

If a child struggles with attention and effort	• Ensure a feeling of success • Consistent maths routines • Narrate maths as the class norm • Ensure a feeling of belonging to a group that does maths
If a child does not understand concepts or procedures	• Explicit instruction • More/better scaffolded practice
If a child cannot recall facts and procedures	• Flashcard work • More/better practice to automaticity • Tailored review questions each lesson

Distinguish between where proficiency is needed and where creativity is needed

There are some tasks in schools that simply need to be completed efficiently and reliably. For example:

- Recording attendance
- Evacuation procedures
- Recording and reporting safeguarding concerns
- Moving a whole class of children from one part of the school to another
- Responding to/escalating inappropriate behaviour

These tasks benefit from constraints to ensure accurate information and ensure safety, but there are also tasks in schools that do not benefit from such constraints. In these instances, it would be more beneficial for leaders to encourage achieving given goals in different ways than insist on restrictive systems. For example:

- Providing feedback to children
- Clearly explaining concepts
- Making children feel as if they belong

Such tasks are not without structure though. Leaders still need to provide parameters, active ingredients (see Chapter 3) or guidance within which to work to maintain cohesion.

Read energy signals and boost when a lull might occur

The school year has a notable pattern of activity. September is a time of optimism following the summer holiday and is filled with the opportunities of a new year. The autumn term is long and, as it gives way to winter, the shorter days and prevalence of illness often result in a lull. The turn of the year sees shorter half terms and more daylight and with spring comes warmer weather. Parents' evenings, reports or preparing for statutory assessment might all contribute to tired colleagues. The summer term has its own challenges of transition, both for children and with teaching colleagues turning their attention to where they might be asked the following academic year. Leaders need to understand the points in time when there might be lulls and attempt to raise energy levels when the time is right.

> **Example**
>
> It is early December and Millie, the headteacher, has a decision to make. She knows that colleagues are tired and there are many demands on their time at this point in the year – testing and data entry, reviewing SEND support plans, the Christmas performances. The next staff meeting is scheduled to provide an opportunity for colleagues to engage in some writing moderation (this had been initially planned at the beginning of the year). From conversations with various colleagues and feedback from other leaders, Millie is certain that the writing moderation for the autumn term is not as important as freeing up some time to use as colleagues see fit. Millie cancels the meeting and instead visits each team briefly at the end of the day to thank them for all their hard work and remind them of the difference they are making to the children.

Understanding your school culture and climate: building knowledge of self

Some of the strategies for building safety, sharing vulnerability and establishing purpose might come more naturally than others. Leaders might be more comfortable doing some than others. Understanding this of themselves is valuable knowledge, but introspection is hard. Leaders probably need to rely on feedback from others to see their blind spots.

Bias is also something to guard against. Leaders might be particularly good at giving belonging cues to some but less so to others. They might share their vulnerability often with some but never with others. They might communicate a clear purpose with some but not with others. Part of building domain-specific knowledge is understanding their own biases (and this is explored more in Chapter 5).

	Reflection prompt	**Seeking feedback**
Building belonging and psychological safety	Which of the belonging cues (above) am I comfortable with giving? Are there any that I am not comfortable giving? Which colleagues do I do these with more than others? Are there any colleagues that I give fewer (or no) belonging cues to?	Tell me about the belonging cues (above) that you have seen me give to others. Are there any that I do not give? Which colleagues do I do these with more? Are there any colleagues that I give fewer (or no) belonging cues to?
Sharing vulnerability	Think of a time when I asked for feedback on the way I handled a situation. Think of a time when I faced an uncomfortable situation head on. Think of a time when I avoided an uncomfortable situation. Think of a time when I organised a debrief of a decision that we made.	Tell me about a time when I asked for feedback on the way I handled a situation. Tell me about a time when I faced an uncomfortable situation head on. Tell me about a time when I avoided an uncomfortable situation. Tell me about a time when I organised a debrief of a decision that we made.

	Reflection prompt	**Seeking feedback**
Establishing purpose	Think of a time when I clearly communicated our direction and priorities.	Tell me about a time when I clearly communicated our direction and priorities.
	What kind of stories do I tell that link the present to the future?	Tell me about the stories I tell that link the present to the future.
	What rules of thumb have I established?	Tell me about any rules of thumb I have established.
	In what situations do I insist on proficiency and in what situations do I encourage creativity?	Tell me about situations where I insist on proficiency and where I encourage creativity.
	Think of a time when I read energy signals and provided a boost to counteract a lull.	Tell me about a time when I read energy signals and provided a boost to counteract a lull.

Understanding your school culture and climate: building knowledge of others

A strong culture and positive climate require more than just *leaders* to build safety, share vulnerability and establish purpose. The more that this is done *by as many colleagues as possible*, the stronger the culture and the more positive the climate. Useful hidden knowledge for leaders includes the extent to which different colleagues build safety, share vulnerability and establish purpose. In any team, there will be some that do these things better than others and, if leaders know the details of this, they could be in a better position to influence the spread of such behaviours. In order to get to know these things, leaders need to listen to and observe interactions. Many of these might be done when no one else is around – heart-warming moments between colleagues unseen by others. As such, leaders rely on the anecdotes of others to know of these valuable interactions. Therefore, asking well-crafted and well-timed questions can help to uncover hidden interactions:

- Think of someone whose company you enjoy at school. What do they do that makes you feel comfortable?
- Think of someone who keeps us focused on doing the right thing at school. What do they do that keeps us on the right track?

Psychological safety does not necessarily come from each individual's interactions with leaders but from interactions they have with those with whom they work the closest. The first layer of belonging that colleagues will feel is to the team in which they spend most of their time – those they work with in their classroom, their year team or their key stage, depending on the size of the school. Therefore, leaders should pay appropriate attention to each network and seek to influence the belonging cues that each individual experiences.

Sometimes, leaders might also need to seek out negative interactions. It might be that an individual's actions are contributing to others feeling psychologically unsafe – isolation instead of belonging. One problem in identifying this is that truth doesn't always rise to the top. The more senior a leader is, the less likely they are to see negative interactions for themselves, as anyone prone to doing it will often keep them private. Leaders need to understand that what they see around the school is probably not the reality of the culture and climate that exists and that, more likely, each colleague will experience a slightly different climate depending on who they work with.

Using knowledge of high performing teams for self-improvement

Leaders have a moral and professional obligation to improve themselves and having better interactions certainly has the potential to be a marginal gain to achieve a stronger culture, a more positive climate and, in turn, better outcomes for children.

> **Example**
>
> Sallie, the assistant headteacher, has realised that she gives far more belonging cues to some colleagues than she does to others and that, as a senior leader, she needs to address this imbalance. She has selected two related behaviours that she thinks would be good to work on, based on her reflections and the feedback she has received from the headteacher: asking questions to draw others out and preventing interruptions. She feels that she often dominates conversations and waits for pauses in conversations so that she can say what she needs to say. She has decided to involve colleagues that she has fewer interactions with in her day-to-day problem solving, asking what they think and resisting the temptation to interrupt with what she is thinking.

Using knowledge of high performing teams to support others to improve

The more that leaders develop a shared mental model of culture and climate, the better placed they are to support the widespread improvement of culture and climate.

> **Example**
>
> Robert, the deputy headteacher, has realised that there is a particular area to work on with the year leaders – tackling uncomfortable truths head on. The year leaders are relatively inexperienced and there have been times when they have avoided tackling uncomfortable situations and climate has been negatively affected. Robert talks year leaders through an example of an 'open to learning conversation' that the team could analyse together. He emphasises the importance of describing concerns as a hypothesis to be checked rather than presenting them as truth, inviting the other person's opinion, establishing common ground and making a plan to get what both want. Robert presents some scenarios for year leaders to practice and encourages them to talk through with him a planned conversation when they next have to have one.

Amplify anecdotes to drive others' behaviour

Amplifying anecdotes of cohesive teams is a great way of influencing the cultural norms. Share them regularly and widely.

> **Example**
>
> Kiran, the headteacher, has chosen to amplify stories around celebrating humble tasks. After a concert for parents finishes, she asks for parents' help in stacking chairs and is pleased to see all the colleagues in attendance doing the same thing. In her thank you email celebrating the event that she sends to all colleagues, she adds: 'Finally, it was wonderful to see how thoughtful everyone was at the end by stacking and putting away the chairs. This is really important to us because our school is built upon such acts of kindness and helpfulness'.

Chapter summary

- The highest performing teams in various domains build safety, share vulnerability and establish purpose.
- Strategies to build safety:
  - Show warmth and kindness in every interaction
  - Give good eye contact
  - Engage in frequent, energetic exchanges
  - Close physical proximity (but not too close)

- Prevent interruptions
- Eat together
- Encourage humour and laughter
- Treat individuals as unique and valued
- Give small attentive courtesies
- Show that you care
- Make mixing happen
- Ask questions to draw others out
- Celebrate the humblest of tasks
- Narrate others' role in the future
- Create connections between people

- Strategies to share vulnerability
  - Seek feedback
  - Face uncomfortable truths head on
  - Debrief decision-making

- Strategies to establish purpose
  - Overcommunicate vision, values and strategic priorities
  - Narrate a link between the present and a future ideal
  - Establish vivid, memorable rules of thumb
  - Distinguish between where proficiency is needed and where creativity is needed
  - Read energy signals and boost when a lull might occur

References

1. Coyle, D. (2019). *Culture code*. London: Random House Business.
2. Kerr, J. (2013). *Legacy*. London: Constable.
3. Robinson, V. (2018). *Reduce change to increase improvement*. Thousand Oaks, CA: Corwin.

5 The power of expectations

Introduction

Teachers' expectations of children have long been known to have a significant effect on their achievement, but what if leaders' expectations of colleagues had a similar (positive or negative) effect on their performance? This chapter looks closely at the specific behaviours that demonstrate leaders' expectations of others and sets them within a number of school-based examples. It explores what leaders might need to do to notice and change their biases and provides multiple prompts to build their hidden knowledge of their and other leaders' expectations of colleagues in their school.

The Pygmalion effect

In 1968, Robert Rosenthal and Lenore Jacobsen embarked on a study[1]. They explained to teachers that, after some testing, they had identified certain children who were destined to bloom intellectually in the year ahead. IQ tests before and at a later point in time showed statistically significant improvements for these children in the first and second grades. The bloomers in all other age groups also improved, albeit not significantly. The twist was that the children who had been identified by the researchers had *not* shown promise on a test. They had just been randomly selected. The conclusion was simple. Teachers' expectations of children can influence their achievement. The researchers were of the opinion that teachers' subconscious behaviours towards children encouraged their success, that believing these children's futures were bright influenced their interactions with these children.

They also hypothesised that the opposite was true, too – that having low expectations of children can lead to poor achievement. Lower expectations manifest as behaviours that provide comparatively fewer opportunities for children to learn.

Can leaders change their biases?

Criticism of the study was related to reliability issues, and some might argue that it is difficult, if not impossible, to address one's own unconscious biases. Nevertheless, a sensible conclusion is that, even if teachers' expectations (and their resultant behaviours) do not affect children's learning, they might well make children feel noticed, reassured and as if they belong. These are all absolutely valid outcomes that teachers might seek to have on children.

What if leaders' expectations of colleagues affect their performance?

The interesting question for school leaders is the extent to which the findings on teachers' expectations of children might translate to the relationship between leaders and their colleagues. What if leaders' expectations of colleagues could affect their performance? If there were similar positive effects that were possible, leaders paying attention to how their expectations are communicated would be a great example of marginal gains – small yet significant improvements that can lead to much greater outcomes. If leaders' expectations of colleagues influence the quality of teaching, it is certainly worth their effort to pay close attention to their words and actions, but, even if the outcomes were a stronger sense of belonging, a greater commitment to the school or staff retention, the time spent would be worth it.

How leaders communicate their expectations

Leaders' expectations are more complex than simply what is said from leader to colleague. Expectations are communicated powerfully not only through what leaders say but also the context of those conversations, including non-verbal signals. The extent to which leaders pay attention to colleagues is an indicator of the expectations they have of them:

- Eye contact
- Proximity
- Warmth

These behaviours demonstrate care and interest in others. There are unlikely to be good rules of thumb for how much of each is appropriate, not least because of cultural differences and individual preferences about what is acceptable. However, these behaviours do seem to be prerequisites to quality interactions between leaders and colleagues, of which there are several considerations:

- Frequency of interaction
- Length of interaction
- Providing more response opportunities for colleagues

More and longer interactions seem to demonstrate higher expectations of others, with the opposite also true. When interactions are more frequent, it increases the opportunity for higher quality content of discussion and support, namely:

- Giving more challenging work and related support
- Giving more and better feedback
- Giving more praise and recognition

Raising your expectations

If leaders' expectations really can make a difference to colleagues' performance, or at least contribute to a positive climate, the crucial consideration is whether they can raise their expectations of colleagues and, in turn, influence their behaviour. Chapter 1 described the importance of underlying beliefs in driving behaviour, so leaders might need to recognise and modify their assumptions about colleagues in order for any behaviour change towards them to manifest. But how?

In a meta-analysis of studies into teachers' expectations of children[2], researchers found that teachers needed to see the achievements of children and have differences in their behaviours pointed out to them, along with the effect of those expectations on children. If these conclusions are applicable to leaders' expectations of colleagues, then there are two important activities that leaders might engage in: amplifying the successes of others and learning about their own biases.

Amplify others' successes

When one notices others being successful, it is important to share it, particularly with other leaders. Doing so encourages positive interactions and, crucially here, could modify others' expectations of the colleague whose success might otherwise have gone unnoticed.

> **Example**
>
> Ayaz is a lower key stage 2 phase leader and is keen to make sure all in the team are aware of what each other is capable of. At the beginning of each team meeting, he sets aside a couple of minutes for one of the team to share a success they have noticed in the team. This week, Ayaz is particularly excited to share his story: 'Earlier this week, I was

called out to take a phone call and my TA (Jan) had to cover for just under half an hour. When I came back to the class, I was ready to apologise and pick up from where we left off. But Jan had the class in the palm of her hand, having reviewed what we had done in the last few lessons, explained the task for them and set them off. She did an amazing job with no notice!'

Learning about your own biases

If it is indeed possible for leaders to notice their biases and make positive changes to their behaviour, it is certain that they'll need a combination of self-reflection and feedback from others. It would also be very important for leaders to understand *how* their expectations are communicated. The chain of conditions by which leaders demonstrate their expectations is quite simple:

- Increased attentiveness to others leads to
- Better interactions with them and creates the opportunity for
- Better substance of conversations.

Example

Charlotte is a headteacher whose office is near the main entrance of the school. When she leaves her office to walk around the school, the first classrooms that she comes to are the year 4 classes. Other year groups are further away. She notices that, because of their proximity to her office, she interacts more with the year 4 team than with the others. In fact, she sees very little of the year 1 team who are based the furthest away and has fewer interactions with them than with any other team.

Leaders are all biased

Bias is inevitable because leaders are human. Everyone will have preferences for who they interact with more than others. These are noticeable to others and the implications of unconscious bias are that leaders might demonstrate higher or lower expectations of different colleagues. Some might perceive leaders to have favourites, or indeed the opposite, based on observed interactions. This may well be unintended on leaders' part but demonstrates the interplay between underlying beliefs, espoused values and behavioural artifacts in Schein's model of culture.

Remember, issues arise when there is disharmony between the levels. A leader who talks about equality and fairness but whose actions demonstrate contrary beliefs is first and foremost human, but such tension between words and behaviours can be detrimental for school culture.

Understanding your school culture and climate: building knowledge of self

If leaders know how their expectations of different colleagues seem to be unbalanced, if they are aware of their biases, then it may be possible to modify their behaviours in order to positively affect culture and climate. This is easier said than done, perhaps because bias is often seen as unconscious; they have to assume that changing their biases will probably be very difficult. However, if the potential gains of doing so includes colleagues' improved performance and an improved school climate, it is well worth attempting. The first option is to set aside time for reflection using prompts that can be built around the formal knowledge of how expectations are communicated.

How attentive am I?

- Have I spoken to everyone today/this week?
- Have I been to every classroom today/this week?
- Do I acknowledge each person by name, with eye contact, when I see them?
- Do I demonstrate warmth to everyone regularly?
- Has everyone seen me today/this week?

Reflecting on these questions can help leaders to review how attentive they are to different colleagues. Inevitably, there will be some colleagues that leaders are more attentive to than others. This might be through how much they like or identify with them, the effort that others make in seeking out contact with leaders or more simply the physical layout of the school building. Maybe colleagues in further away classrooms from where leaders are based receive less attention and vice versa.

How do I interact with others?

- With whom do I have the most interactions?
- With whom do I have the least interactions?
- Who initiates these interactions?
- With whom do interactions last the longest? Why?

- With whom are interactions the shortest? Why?
- In interactions with each person, who talks more? Why?

There will be all sorts of explanations for the differences realised when answering these questions, some of which follow on from the previous set of prompts. Reflecting this deeply on interactions with colleagues might be time consuming, but, if it develops vital informal knowledge that leaders can then act on to make a difference to others' performance, it is time well spent.

What do I tend to talk about with others?

- What do I talk about with each person?
- What sort of praise or recognition do I offer each person?
- What sort of feedback do I offer each person?
- What sort of feedback do I seek from each person?
- What sort of tasks do I ask of each person?
- What sort of responsibilities do I offer each person?

The responses to these prompts can be fascinating. One might interact with certain colleagues more than others, but the substance of those interactions matters. They may or may not be work related. They may be about what they have been reading or what they have been experimenting with in the classroom. The substance of interactions makes a difference to the leaders' implicit expectations that are communicated to those they interact with. One might find that types of praise and feedback differ between colleagues and then consider it to be unfair that some get 'better' praise and feedback than others.

Seeking feedback does more than simply generate useful information

Self-reflection is one way of developing the informal knowledge that might be needed if leaders are to address their biases and demonstrate high expectations of every colleague. Another is for leaders to deliberately seek feedback about their behaviours and the perceptions of their intent. One of the key components of high performing teams described in Chapter 4 was sharing vulnerability and there is some important nuance here.

Vulnerability in this sense is the opposite of ego protection. Some leaders might have the underlying belief that they are the font of all knowledge and are solely responsible for problem solving. They might believe that asking for help is a sign of weakness, fearing the perception of incompetence or indecisiveness. Sharing vulnerability operates from the assumption that leaders' ideas about solving problems are hypotheses to be tested rather than established truths; that one person's judgement alone is unlikely to appreciate the range of factors influencing a problem. The implications of leaders' vulnerability are significant for climate. There can be fewer interactions that show leaders' appreciation of colleagues' expertise than the leader asking 'What do you think?'.

Leaders need feedback on how their bias manifests. Even the leader most dedicated to self-improvement and working diligently on self-reflection will miss their blind spots. Asking what others think is a starting point, but there are other questions that might yield useful information for leaders.

One option is an anonymous survey. Depending on relationships, it could be more likely that leaders will get more accurate information if names are dissociated from responses. But respondents will need a structure to ensure that the most useful information is received. For example, leaders might pose the following prompt:

> Think about the interactions you have with me or you see me have with others. What should I start doing? What should I stop doing? What should I continue doing?

This start, stop, continue framework can prompt a range of feedback about what's going well and what's not. The information gathered here might be useful and it might make receiving more accurate feedback more likely because of anonymity, but it lacks something important. It lacks connection with others.

Part of the power of sharing vulnerability is the relationships that are developed simply through being vulnerable. Finding out about how others perceive the way in which leaders interact also provides them with useful informal knowledge. They might pose certain questions to each colleague about their interactions to better develop their informal knowledge of their experiences and, in turn, tailor those interactions in an attempt to make them better. They might also gather feedback on how other leaders perceive their interactions with colleagues. The result is not only the discovery of useful informal knowledge but also the development of a positive climate due to the nature of the interactions themselves.

How attentive do I appear to be?

Ask other leaders:

- Tell me about my eye contact and warmth when I interact with others. Do I appear to treat everyone equally?
- Tell me about parts of the school/colleagues that I visit the most/least.

Ask each individual:

- Do you see enough of me around school?

How do I interact with others?

Ask other leaders:

- With whom do I have the most/least interactions?
- Who initiates these interactions?
- With whom do interactions last the longest/shortest?
- In my interactions with others, who talks more?

What do I tend to talk about with others?

Ask each individual:

- Tell me about the balance between work and non-work conversations that we have. Is this about right?
- Do you get enough praise and recognition from me?
- What kind of praise and recognition works best for you?
- Do you get enough developmental feedback from me?
- What kind of developmental feedback is most useful to you?

Find out others' preferences

It might be that different colleagues have different preferences when it comes to interactions with leaders. Some might want or need far more regular interactions than others. What's important is that leaders provide the kind of praise and feedback that seems to be most effective for each individual. Some colleagues may have the underlying assumption that if leaders don't bring up work-related issues with them, then everything to do with their performance is fine and they are doing a good job. Others might have the underlying assumption that if leaders don't bring up work-related issues with them, then something must be wrong. Knowing each colleague's assumptions should determine the type and substance of interactions instigated by leaders.

Understanding your school culture and climate: building knowledge of others

Leaders might decide to frame these questions differently depending on circumstances. The headteacher, for example, due to their role as the figurehead and the importance of this for culture and climate, might want to seek feedback about their interactions with others. Relationships between the headteacher and every colleague are vital for a positive environment. However, it might also be valid that, in large schools, with so many colleagues, this is not possible. Instead, one might seek feedback about leaders' interactions with everyone else more generally.

How attentive are leaders?

- Tell me about eye contact and warmth when leaders interact with others. Do leaders appear to treat everyone equally?
- Tell me about parts of the school/colleagues that leaders visit the most/least.
- Do you see enough of leaders around the school?

How do leaders interact with others?

- Who do leaders have the most/least interactions with?
- Who initiates these interactions with leaders?
- With whom do leaders' interactions last the longest/shortest?
- In interactions with others, do leaders talk more or listen more?

What do leaders tend to talk about with others?

- Tell me about the balance between work and non-work conversations that leaders have with others. Is this about right?
- Do you get enough praise and recognition from leaders?
- Do you get enough developmental feedback from leaders?

Using knowledge of expectations for self-improvement

If leaders' expectations improve colleagues' performance, it is certainly worth them deliberately becoming more attentive by having more frequent and higher quality interactions.

> **Example**
>
> Jeremy is an upper key stage 2 phase leader with a team of four teachers and six teaching assistants. His own reflections on his biases were confirmed by the colleagues from whom he asked for feedback – he is attentive and has good interactions with the teachers in his team but not the teaching assistants, with the exception of Jibraeel, who works in his class. Jeremy knows that addressing this starts with attentiveness, so he spends the next week or so simply making sure that he greets each teaching assistant every day with warmth and good eye contact and that they come into contact regularly. The next week, Jeremy extends these interactions, asking each TA their opinion on various issues and asking them for help with things such as how the six TAs might be deployed better across the four classes. With more developed relationships with each TA now established, Jeremy sets about digging deeper into their preferences to do with work. He explains that he wants to get praise and feedback right for them and enquires about what type works well for them and how regularly. In subsequent weeks of the phase, he carefully chooses successes to recognise and developmental feedback to offer to suit the preferences of each colleague.

Using knowledge of expectations to support others to improve

A collective mental model of expectations of different colleagues is well worth developing through discussion and pattern seeking. The information gathered can lead to feedback that is more valid if the same inferences are made by multiple colleagues.

> **Example**
>
> Mamuna, a headteacher, wants to gather her senior leadership team's feedback on the expectations that they have collectively of others. She asks them which colleague gets most of their attention and which are tasked with additional responsibilities. It soon becomes clear that one of the leadership team, Jane, talks almost exclusively about one colleague out of a total of 15 teachers. Further feedback from others suggests that this is a common occurrence. Mamuna is worried about a) the workload implications of the teacher that Jane talks about the most and b) the perception that this teacher is the favourite. The leadership team discusses the possible implications on climate and Mamuna offers Jane advice, which Jane agrees with. Jane needs to reach out to other colleagues more often and spend less time interacting with the person that seems to dominate her attention. Mamuna helps Jane to map out what she is planning to talk to this colleague about and suggests others that she might interact with instead to complete the work that she needs to do.

Amplify anecdotes to drive others' behaviour

Telling stories of positive examples is a great way to draw attention to and encourage the kind of behaviour that leaders want to see more of.

> **Example**
>
> Naveed is a deputy headteacher and wants to draw attention to the biases that leaders might have and what they might do about it. Naveed has realised that most leaders give feedback based on their own preferences and wants them to consider the preferences of their colleagues before deciding on how to give feedback on performance. Naveed knows that one of the year leaders, Pearl, has had success with this because one of the teachers in Pearl's team came and told him about it: 'Naveed, I have to tell you about something that happened last week. I've had lesson feedback hundreds of times over the years and I never really paid much attention to it. Someone usually comes in, suggests that I do something that doesn't make much sense because they haven't seen the previous lessons, and that's the end of it. This time with Pearl though it was different. We met beforehand and she asked me what kind of feedback would be useful. I told her that I'd find it useful if she could tell me at the time what she thinks I could do to improve so that I could try and do it straight away, in the moment. When Pearl watched my lesson, she suggested a better way to check for understanding. I tried it there and then and noticed that some children had struggled when I probably wouldn't have noticed that before. It was a great experience!'
>
> Naveed is pleased to hear this. At the next leadership meeting, he explains that he has great news to share and sets the scene, before asking Pearl to explain what she did. Naveed is quick to point out that it is not the live coaching that is important, but the fact that Pearl had sought the kind of feedback that her colleague would find useful. The other year leaders find it interesting and a conversation follows about the importance of asking people what kind of feedback is most useful to them.

Chapter summary

- Leaders' expectations of colleagues could influence their performance.
- Leaders all have biases that manifest in how they treat colleagues.
- How colleagues are treated determines how they feel individually and collectively determine the climate.
- Non-verbal signals, as well as the substance of interactions, demonstrate leaders' expectations of others.
- Attentiveness matters | Eye contact, proximity, warmth.

- Attentiveness is a prerequisite for interactions.
- Interactions matter | Frequency, length, plenty of response opportunities.
- More interactions are necessary but not sufficient for better substance in conversation.
- Substance matters | Challenge, support, feedback.

References

1. Rosenthal, R., & Jacobson, L. (1968). 'Pygmalion in the classroom'. The Urban Review, 3(1), 16–20. DOI: 10.1007/bf02322211
2. de Boer, Hester, Timmermans, Anneke C., & van der Werf, Margaretha P.C. (2018). 'The effects of teacher expectation interventions on teachers' expectations and student achievement: narrative review and meta-analysis'. Educational Research and Evaluation, 24(3–5), 180–200. DOI: 10.1080/13803611.2018.1550834

Harnessing the drivers of motivation

Introduction

A motivated team can achieve great things. This chapter applies the idea that motivation results from the team experiencing a feeling of autonomy, mastery and purpose. Although this work was carried out in the business domain, there are clear applications to school leadership, which are exemplified across a range of roles and school-based scenarios. It explores the tension of how many established school practices prevent autonomy and mastery, despite the universal human need for these conditions, providing leaders with prompts to build their hidden knowledge of how these issues of culture and climate manifest in their school.

Success breeds motivation

It can be tempting to believe that leaders need to motivate their team. Indeed, it is common for school leadership adverts to describe the candidate being sought as someone who can do just that. The assumption is that if a leader motivates their team, then success will follow.

The reality is quite the opposite.

Motivation is better thought of as an outcome – part of the climate. People feel motivated when they feel successful. Motivation is certainly a desirable outcome and a motivated team is likely to reinforce a positive climate and productive culture. Leaders might not be able to directly motivate their teams, but motivation is the result of a combination of factors over which leaders do have control. If school leaders seek a motivated staff, it is not about rousing speeches but about creating working conditions that ensure colleagues succeed. Success in schools takes many forms and the more successful colleagues feel, the more likely they are to invest attention and effort in similar opportunities in the future.

Daniel Pink described three drivers of motivation: autonomy, mastery and purpose[1]. Pink examined how decades-old studies provided a glimpse of what is wrong with managers' conception of motivation in the business world. He argued that this is fundamentally at odds with what it means to be human and, as such, its application to school leadership is worth looking into.

Autonomy

It is important for colleagues to have control over how they spend their time, but this can make some school leaders feel uneasy when they are under pressure for the school to meet various standards. It might be an Ofsted grade or the proportion of children attaining certain thresholds at the end of each key stage. In attempting to bring order to the incredible complexity of school life, leaders might aim to control what colleagues do. Leaders will often have a clear idea of what it is that they want – a mental model of how schools should run – and seek to impose that in their school. They will advocate particular practices and might take the view that everyone needs to be carrying out these practices in order for the school to be successful.

If leaders want a positive climate, they need to prioritise autonomy. But this doesn't mean that leaders should simply allow colleagues free reign over what they do and how they do it. Doing so may result in an experience of inconsistency and incoherence for children. Of course, leaders have to provide direction. This tension between knowing that autonomy is important and needing to develop a shared understanding of the job and what it entails is where leadership expertise makes the difference to school culture and climate. Too far in the control direction and culture may well create consistency but to the detriment of climate. Too far in the other direction and leaders risk an incoherent culture. Increasing autonomy can work if colleagues are well trained and have a strong shared purpose.

Interestingly, the actual autonomy that colleagues experience seems to matter less than how they perceive it. NFER research[2] into teacher autonomy in 2020 found that perceived autonomy is strongly associated with improved job satisfaction and a greater intention to stay in teaching. The issue for leaders to understand is what teachers need to feel autonomy over. Four elements of autonomy for leaders to consider are task, time, technique and team.

Before we examine these, it is worth considering a metaphor for autonomy. Imagine an autonomy continuum. At one extreme, there is little or no autonomy for colleagues. At the other extreme, there is full autonomy. The former is characterised by controlling leaders, lists of non-negotiables and the like. It would be tempting to think that the other end has its flaws too. And it does. But they are not necessarily flaws that result in a negative climate like at the other end of the continuum. The main consideration for leaders must be to maximise autonomy – to push it as far to the extreme as they can – all the while providing a combination of clear direction (see Chapter 3) about what the school is trying to achieve, what the team values and the active ingredients of great teaching with training that builds expertise and enables action. It is this work by leaders that creates the right blend of overall cohesion and autonomy. Colleagues will need to feel autonomy over what they do (task), how they organise their time, how they complete their tasks and with whom they work.

Autonomy over task

No matter the job role in schools, there will be main responsibilities that each colleague has. Take curriculum content. Providing teachers with choice over what they teach might improve their perception of autonomy but carries with it the risk of compromising a well-sequenced curriculum over year groups and key stages. An appropriate trade off might be for leaders to involve teachers in curriculum design collaboratively at the strategic level if they have an interest or expertise in a particular subject.

Teachers' main responsibility of planning and teaching lessons is standard, but there are other aspects of school work that leaders might enable for interested colleagues. Developing expertise in another aspect of school work is an opportunity that leaders should create. This might be subject leadership, the work of the SENDCo, or how a school runs from an operational perspective.

> **Example**
>
> Emma is a deputy headteacher and, through discussions with teachers, she knows that a colleague (Khalid) is developing an interest in supporting children from disadvantaged backgrounds. Emma is keen to support Khalid's interest because a) it would benefit the school to have more colleagues with expertise in this area and b) it is a source of motivation for Khalid. Emma signposts Khalid to some research, blog posts and podcasts on the subject and signs him up to a course on the effective use of the pupil premium that is being run locally.

Autonomy over time

While teachers have to be in school when children are there, leaders have the opportunity to afford autonomy over starting and finishing times. Some colleagues may prefer an early start, while others prefer a later finish. Leaders can get it wrong when they stipulate times that colleagues need to be in school – for example, that nobody can leave before 4pm. In one school where this was the rule, it was not uncommon for teachers to sit talking for ten minutes, coats on and car keys in hand ready to leave at 4pm on the dot. Far better to understand that individuals have unique home lives and patterns of productivity. Taking into account family commitments and affording flexibility about when tasks are done is an important contributor to climate.

What about during the school day? Teachers' timetables are central to their perceived autonomy. There will of course be constraints, as rooms might need to be shared or access to specialists, plus the availability of cover for PPA. Other aspects of the timetable are more open to informed choice, such as when subjects are taught and for how long. The latter is a bug bear. Hour-long lessons are a hangover from the national strategies in the early 2000s and do not have to dictate timetabling. This kind of autonomy can only be fruitful when leaders provide clear direction – for example, keeping teachers focused on intended curricula outcomes for children and encouraging decision-making in the best interests of the children in their classes. Children need to get up and move? Do it. A lesson going really well and worth extending to explore ideas further? Do it. A lesson not going well and needs rethinking? Scrap it and do something else. Leaders need to say these things out loud, thereby normalising this kind of decision-making.

It is important for leaders to ensure breadth of experience, though, and it would be tempting to 'check' that the timetable is actually happening: 'Does year 5 do geography on a Tuesday afternoon?' This is a mistake that could encourage compliance to the detriment of children's learning. Far better to routinely talk to children about what they are learning in each subject and talk to teachers about how the teaching of each subject is going. Any issues around breadth can be explored to find solutions.

Autonomy over technique

How people perform their main responsibilities is a significant factor in the perception of autonomy. It is not uncommon for leaders to dictate how teachers should teach, telling them exactly how time in lessons should be spent on which activities – for example, mandating retrieval practice at the beginning of every lesson or writing a learning objective on the board for children to copy. It is understandable why some leaders choose to do the former. Perhaps they have had success with particular strategies, perhaps there is a lack of shared understanding about what constitutes great teaching in the school, or perhaps the leader wants to make more use of evidence-informed approaches. While this might provide the comfort blanket of 'consistency' (albeit superficial), the negative effect on motivation through the removal of autonomy cannot be ignored.

The tension between autonomy and guidance from leaders can be alleviated by leaders specifying the active ingredients of the school's teaching strategy and the principles and actions that make the chosen strategy most likely to be effective.

> **Example**
>
> Michelle is an assistant headteacher and responsible for reviewing the marking and feedback policy. Feedback from teachers and senior leaders' reflections on the current policy match up – it is too restrictive, dictating how and how often teachers should be marking

> and feeding back on work with little consideration for whether children are in the early stages of key stage 1 or nearing the end of key stage 2. Michelle knows that this is an area where they could provide more autonomy, so she suggests a different approach. Michelle leads colleagues to think about the active ingredients of a feedback strategy rather than listing specific practices. Colleagues agree that children of different ages will certainly require different approaches, as will children of the same age but different expertise. Appropriate feedback in different subjects will also differ, so blanket approaches are certain to be ineffective. Michelle gives teachers a couple of weeks to think about which approaches seem to be useful to children and manageable for teachers. When they meet again, they supplement the policy with some examples that teachers can select from when choosing how to provide feedback.

It is training where perception of autonomy seems to be particularly important. When teachers have autonomy over their professional development goals, they report higher job satisfaction[2]. When there is a lack of autonomy here, teachers turn up to training on INSET days or twilights that leaders have sketched out for the year. Leaders will have chosen multiple areas to focus on depending on the different priorities vying for attention at different points of the year. Expert and novice teachers alike might attend the same session and receive the same messages. In counter to this, leaders must provide opportunities for the team to follow their areas of interest at the level of their own prior knowledge and, importantly, make sure that this ties in with the overall strategic direction of the school. For example, if reading is a whole school priority, then the way that this manifests for each teacher might differ slightly in terms of what their children need and what their existing level of expertise is. Leaders might set up opportunities for teachers to work on:

- Pedagogy relating to phonics
- Adapting reading lessons to meet the needs of children with SEND
- The step from decoding to fluency
- Building background knowledge
- Text choice
- Reviewing structures of a unit of work for reading
- Improving story time
- Addressing unconscious bias

- Addressing low level disruption

- Working with parents

The challenge for leaders is to support each colleague in identifying where they would like to focus their attention and why within an overall framework that supports school improvement by increasing the expertise of each individual colleague.

Autonomy over team

When teachers spend so much time where they work, it matters that they have some choice over with whom they collaborate. Multi-form entry schools will have year or phase teams that are fixed, but leaders can also encourage connections outside of those teams so that colleagues can work with those they choose. Colleagues can get to know each other and decide for themselves who they might collaborate with on mutually interesting projects.

> **Example**
>
> Faheem, an assistant headteacher, knows how important autonomy is and is aware that, usually, most colleagues do not necessarily get to choose with whom they work. He is keen to create opportunities for colleagues to work outside their year teams with individuals of their choosing. He knows that good collaboration is about working together to achieve a particular goal, so he suggests an idea at a senior leadership meeting early in September: 'Research suggests that having autonomy over professional development goals is important but so is having autonomy over with whom we work. There is an opportunity here to create both. We have our strategic priorities: curriculum development, improving behaviour, raising attainment in reading and reducing a deficit budget. If we use these broad headings as areas for teachers to pursue an interest in, teams will naturally form of likeminded people. Given enough time to think it through, colleagues that do not ordinarily work with one another but want to can match up their professional development goals and have the chance to collaborate'.

Mastery

Pink describes mastery as the desire to get better and better at something that matters. He references Csikszentmihalyi's work on flow, a state where people have clear goals, where the challenge is neither too easy nor too difficult and, as a result, they find it deeply satisfying. A state of flow cannot exist without autonomy. While mastery is the result of years of effort, flow is deep engagement in the moment, where hours seem to pass by in minutes. For colleagues to experience flow:

- Goals need to be clear
- Feedback needs to be immediate
- Challenges need to be neither too easy nor too hard
- They need to have control over it
- They need to be able to concentrate, free from distractions

Colleagues who are engaged in their work, have clear goals and receive timely feedback are primed to experience flow, and it is therefore more likely to exert a greater influence over outcomes for children.

Purpose

As we have seen, a clear purpose is fundamental to a strong culture and positive climate and is also necessary for flow. Chapter 3 describes in more detail the importance of purpose, but Pink's contribution to the concept is to emphasise that purpose needs to be greater and more permanent than the self.

> Autonomous people working toward mastery perform at very high levels. But those who do so in the service of some greater objective can achieve even more[1].

Working in education provides this greater objective – the education of children that will one day be discovering cures for diseases or leading nations, that will grow up to contribute positively to their communities and continue the education of future generations. Purposes do not come much greater. The challenge for school leaders is to harness this – to ensure that colleagues see the woods and not simply the trees.

Pink's three drivers of motivation are very much intertwined and, to make the most of them, school leaders need to provide clear direction while encouraging engagement but reducing the amount of control over colleagues.

Understanding your school culture and climate: building knowledge of self

The way that leaders communicate heavily influences both the climate and the culture, so it is prudent for them to take the time to gather feedback on what they tend to talk about and how they do so. Leaders might know that autonomy is important and talk about the desire for colleagues to have autonomy, yet their actions may contradict their sentiments. Consider the example of a leader who checks on compliance with a marking policy that stipulates how work should be marked. This kind of monitoring is a hangover from a previous Ofsted inspection framework, where certain marking strategies were heralded as indicators of great teaching and could be easily checked by flicking through a few books. This kind of activity is at odds with a true understanding of autonomy and the message sent is louder and clearer than any token soundbite about autonomy. Leaders need to get to know what they talk about and what they do when on autopilot, but this can often be a blind spot. Ask:

- What do I say when I talk about [elements of autonomy, such as] marking/teaching strategies/classroom layout?
- How do I talk about our purpose? What kinds of things do I say?
- Is there anything I do that contradicts what I say is important?

Understanding your school culture and climate: building knowledge of others

A climate where colleagues feel motivated is the aggregation of each individual's perception of their job. It is therefore useful for leaders to know the extent to which each colleague perceives the autonomy they have, the extent to which they experience flow and their reason for choosing education and the leader's school.

Leaders could ask what colleagues feel they have autonomy over in common school practices:

- The content they teach
- How they teach it
- Their timetable
- How they assess
- How they give children feedback
- Their professional development
- How they set up their classroom
- How they manage behaviour

It matters not what leaders think they have provided colleagues autonomy over. What matters is colleagues' perception of that autonomy. Leaders might know, for example, that teachers have autonomy over how they arrange the furniture in their classroom because they have never mandated a particular arrangement. This does not mean that colleagues feel they have autonomy over this aspect of their practice. It might be that it has never been said out loud by leaders that teachers should choose for themselves the best layout for their classroom. Perhaps there is a type of layout that is coincidentally prevalent across the school of tables in blocks of six.

A new colleague might notice this and infer that this is the way tables should be laid out and conform, even though they may disagree. Inadvertently, this colleague might report low autonomy, which would be a surprise to leaders.

The implication for leaders is to regularly find out what colleagues think. This is probably best done through conversation in order to pick up on nuances, but it of course takes time. The reality is that different colleagues will value different aspects of autonomy; some might want absolute control over their teaching strategies while not being too fussed about having autonomy over the content of what they teach, for example. Are there aspects of practice that colleagues feel they have less autonomy over? What about the feeling in different year groups? This data collection alone is insufficient; it is the follow-up that counts. It might be that leaders need to reduce the amount of control over what colleagues do or it might be that they need to communicate more clearly about what the team values and what matters to avoid misconceptions developing.

A positive climate will certainly be one where colleagues experience flow and have a desire to get better. As such, it is worth leaders knowing who experiences it and who doesn't so that they can tweak conditions accordingly. Remember, a feeling of flow requires a clear goal, timely feedback and just the right amount of challenge alongside a feeling of competence. Again, conversations with individuals are a great way to find this out. Leaders might ask:

- Tell me about what you are trying to achieve at work.
- Do you get enough developmental feedback? What kind of feedback works best for you?
- What aspects of your role do you feel good at? Are there any aspects you don't feel good at?

Leaders might be tempted to collect this information at scale with surveys, but this could be a mistake. Reducing the responses to options on a Likert scale is unlikely to provide useful enough information and, as we saw in Chapter 5, the conversation itself builds relationships. Leaders need to take the time to have the conversations with preferably all colleagues.

Perhaps most importantly, a positive climate is dependent on colleagues' understanding of purpose. Chapter 3 looked at this idea in detail and this chapter has shown how necessary a clear purpose is for colleagues to feel motivated. Leaders not only need to overcommunicate the purpose but seek out others' understanding of it. Leaders can be rather influential in weaving a narrative about who they are and what they do, but each colleague will interpret that based on their own prior knowledge and motivations, and they will quite predictably come to their own understanding of it.

Knowing this helps leaders to adapt the stories they tell in order to focus attention around the common purpose. In seeking this understanding, it might be tempting for leaders to look out for the language that others use when they talk about a given issue and check the extent to which this matches the wording used when they initially set out their strategic direction. However, this approach runs the risk of colleagues telling leaders what they think they want to hear.

> **Example**
>
> Max, a headteacher, wants to know the extent to which his team understands the school's purpose and values. There are certain words that Max uses regularly to talk about this, but he isn't interested in colleagues parroting these back to him. He wants to hear what colleagues have to say in their own words. Max starts off conversations by asking about what the school stands for and what makes it unique. Max finds the conversations fascinating. Not only does he learn a little more about each individual, but the way that they explain what the school means is sometimes better than he had articulated himself years previously. In fact, Max begins to collate these explanations to form the next iteration of how he'll publicise the purpose and strategic direction of the school.

Using the knowledge of motivation for self-improvement

> **Example**
>
> Monika, an assistant headteacher, has identified that an area she could be better at is creating conditions that enable others to experience flow. She knows that, for this to happen, colleagues need clear goals, to be free from distraction and receive timely feedback. Monika has been working with teachers on improving the clarity of their modelling and explanations in teaching writing and believes she can make more of a difference to others' motivation by building in clearer goals, removing distractions and providing better feedback. She meets with Pablo, a year 2 teacher, to plan an upcoming lesson.
>
> Monika: 'Pablo, as you know, we're looking to improve the clarity of modelling and explanations in reading. Have you had a chance to think about a specific goal?'
>
> Pablo replies with a vague answer about modelling the opening of a story.
>
> Monika: 'That's a great start. In the opening to this story, are there any particular elements of writing that you want to model? What's the key message that you want to get across?'
>
> Pablo thinks for a minute and suggests it would be good if children could grab the reader's attention in the story opening.
>
> Monika: 'Agreed, an attention-grabbing opening is important. In the version that you model, how will you demonstrate grabbing the reader's attention?'

> Pablo isn't sure at first and looks through some of the examples of openings that he has shown to the children. He notices one particular strategy that is common – the characters are immediately in the middle of the action.
>
> Monika: 'Great idea. Let's map out together the modelled writing that you'll do with the class and rehearse the explanation'.

Using knowledge of motivation to support others to improve

> **Example**
>
> A deputy headteacher, Mia, gathers information through lots of conversations about her colleagues' perception of autonomy. She finds a pocket of discontent in year 5, where it appears that the year leader (Shabana) has been overly prescriptive when requesting planning from colleagues to share with the team. Mia asks to meet Shabana to discuss her concerns.
>
> Mia: 'Thanks for meeting with me, Shabana. I know you're busy and I appreciate the time. Listen, I think I have come across a concern, but I wanted to check it out with you first to see if I have got it right. It's to do with what you're expecting of the year 5 team in terms of the detail of the planning. I get the feeling that what they are expected to produce is quite prescriptive. Do you see it differently?'
>
> Shabana explains that she has indeed asked for quite prescriptive plans because some of the plans she has received from others have been quite patchy and she has had to spend time adding to them on top of producing her own plans to share with the team.
>
> Mia: 'Okay, let me check that I have understood. Some of the plans that others give you are not detailed enough for you to use. Is that right?'
>
> Shabana agrees, adding that it increased her workload so much that she had to change the way the team worked. She knows that others have been frustrated by it.
>
> Mia: 'I agree that it is really important to share plans that can be used by others without too much additional work. I also think that having autonomy over planning is important. What do you think?'
>
> Shabana agrees and suggests that maybe some work can be done as a whole school on planning that balances the need to be used by others with the need for autonomy over how plans are made.

Amplify anecdotes about motivation to drive others' behaviour

> **Example**
>
> Aneesah, a key stage 1 leader, wants to promote autonomy over classroom layout. In her team, one of the teachers (Polly) is less experienced and Aneesah has noticed that she tends to mimic how her classroom is organised, including table arrangement, carpet space and storage of resources. She decides to tackle this in a team meeting. 'I'd like to talk about classroom layout. I have chosen to have a carpet space for children to all come together for when I am explaining things because it helps me to check their attention and understanding'. She turns to anther experienced teacher (Ali) and asks him to explain why he has chosen not to have a carpet space. Ali explains that he feels his class benefits more from fewer transitions between carpet and seats. He adds that his classroom is slightly smaller and therefore having a carpet space would make furniture arrangement cramped. 'Great', says Aneesah. 'It is important that we're making choices about how our classrooms are arranged based on our individual circumstances'. The next day, Aneesah follows up with Polly to begin the conversation about the best furniture arrangement for her class.

Chapter summary

- The direction of influence between motivation and success is counterintuitive.
- People experience motivation when they feel successful.
- Leaders cannot motivate others, only contribute to conditions that might result in motivation.
- Motivation requires autonomy.
- People need autonomy over what they do, how they do it, when they do it and with whom they do it.
- Teachers' perception of autonomy affects how they feel about work.
- Motivation requires mastery.
- Mastery is the desire to get better at something that matters.
- Mastery is dependent on people experiencing flow – a clear goal, timely feedback and just the right amount of challenge.

- Motivation requires purpose.

- Purpose frames what people do in the pursuit of something bigger than themselves.

References

1. Pink, D. (2009). *Drive: the surprising truth about what motivates us.* New York: Riverhead Books.
2. Worth, Jack, & Van den Brande, Jens. (2018). *Teacher autonomy: how does it relate to job satisfaction and retention?* National Foundation for Educational Research. www.nfer.ac.uk/teacher-autonomy-how-does-it-relate-to-job-satisfaction-and-retention.

High levels of trust are required to improve outcomes for children

Introduction

Trust is a desirable condition, but it is not simply nice to have. A school community that trusts each other is far more likely to be successful, while an absence of trust condemns a school to failure. This chapter combines findings about trust in schools with recognised elements of trusting relationships from other domains to provide a model for understanding and influencing how trust supports school leaders to improve their schools. Trustworthiness is such a desirable trait that all leaders will have blind spots regarding their own behaviours and the extent to which they influence trust, so this chapter provides a number of ways to reveal those behaviours so that leaders can make deliberate efforts to influence a more trusting climate.

> Trust is the confidence among team members that their peers' intentions are good, and that there is no reason to be protective or careful around the group. In essence, teammates must get comfortable being vulnerable with one another.
>
> *Lencioni[1]*

The importance of trust

It is hardly ground-breaking to suggest that a positive climate is one where colleagues trust each other, but trust can do more than influence the climate. Research has revealed that schools where high trust is evident between colleagues, children and families are three times more likely to improve children's outcomes[2]. Moreover, they found next to no schools improving outcomes where low trust was evident. Bryk and Schneider showed that trust was not only nice to have, it was also a prerequisite for student achievement.

This source regarding the importance of trust comes from educational research, but there is plenty in other domains that can be useful for school leaders too.

Lencioni's work on the five dysfunctions of teams[1] places trust as the foundation of teamwork, where it allows for other productive team behaviours to support a team to flourish:

- They trust one another, and this trust is rooted in vulnerability.
- They engage in unfiltered conflict around ideas.
- They commit to decisions and plans of action.
- They hold one another accountable for delivering against those plans.
- They focus on the achievement of collective results.

Culture and climate are two sides of the same coin

Lencioni's model mostly describes culture – how people behave – but it acknowledges that the climate (trust) is essential for teams to be functional rather than dysfunctional. Culture and climate are two sides of the same coin, both influencing the other with neither being 'first'. Indeed, it is important for leaders to understand that building trust is not an independent endeavour:

> Leadership is not just about building trust. Nor is it only about getting the work done. It is about doing both of those things simultaneously.
> *Viviane Robinson*[3]

School leaders require a mental model of what trust is and how it is built that will enable them to build trusting relationships while tackling the unique manifestation of the persistent problems of school leadership.

Character and competence

In his bestselling book *The speed of trust*,[4] Covey describes trust as a function of character and competence. Feltman[5] recognises the same characteristics but names them as behavioural and moral. Character (moral choices) is rooted in integrity and intention, while competence (behavioural choices) is based on capabilities and results. To trust someone, we must know that the other person is honest and truly cares as well as be assured that they have the required expertise to do their job well and have a track record of doing so.

Sliding doors moments

Trust is built through many, many seemingly insignificant interactions. Each one, as Dr John Gottman[6] describes them, is a sliding doors moment where one can demonstrate an act of trust or the opposite, an act of betrayal. Each interaction could very well take a relationship down a different path. For school leaders developing their culture and aiming to improve school climate, these interactions are arguably their most important job – building trust while getting the important work of school improvement done.

Boss competence

Competence and integrity also feature in Bryk and Schneider's attributes to build trust and Tschannen-Moran's faces of trust[7]. Leaders need to know that others' words match their deeds and that they can do their jobs well. Interestingly, it has been shown that a boss's competence is the single strongest predictor of a worker's wellbeing[8] and this concept of competence includes both the boss being able to do the worker's job and the boss having a good understanding of their own job.

Four more key elements of trust

While competence and integrity seem to be common features of different models of trust, there are other behaviours that are no less important when it comes to building trust. This collection of behaviours makes up a school's culture:

- Vulnerability
- Healthy conflict
- Commitment
- Holding to account

Trust requires vulnerability

Perhaps the most important definition of trust includes the role that vulnerability plays in a team pulling in the same direction. Lencioni identifies the following behaviours as features of trusting teams:

- Admitting weaknesses and mistakes
- Accepting questions and input about areas of responsibility

Admit weaknesses and mistakes

To create an environment where colleagues trust leaders enough to be vulnerable, leaders must do so first. This is the first step to setting the norm that leaders all have weaknesses, they all make mistakes and it is acceptable to ask for help. Similarly, offering and accepting apologies without hesitation is a key part of dealing with mistakes.

> **Example**
>
> The year 4 team is meeting to discuss the sequence of learning for geography in the upcoming term. Jenny, the year leader, starts the meeting by explaining what the unit for work is about – mountains. Jenny's teaching partner in year 4 (Asim) has recently joined the school as an early career teacher. 'Asim, geography is not my strongest subject and, although I've taught this unit of work before, I don't think I taught it very well. Children did not seem to grasp the key ideas. Can you have a look at what children should know and understand by the end of the unit and see what you think of the sequence?'

Accept questions and input about areas of responsibility

Not only should leaders be able to do this without adopting a defensive attitude, they should actively encourage questions and feedback. Leaders who appreciate others' expertise and actively seek it out set an example for others to follow.

> **Example**
>
> Tanya is a deputy headteacher at a large primary school. The senior leadership team is made up of the headteacher, another deputy headteacher and an assistant headteacher. Tanya is responsible for inclusion and is also the SENDCo. The senior leadership team is meeting to review SEND provision as part of their usual cycle of quality assurance. The headteacher starts the meeting and encourages the rest of the SLT to share what is working well and what could be better about SEND provision. 'I think we have an issue in year 2. Teachers want too many children added to the SEND register', remarks the assistant headteacher. 'Tanya, do you think that our teachers fully understand their responsibilities set out in the SEND code of practice?' Tanya tells the rest of the team that there is some misunderstanding among teachers about the conditions under which a child is added to the SEND register and asks if others have noticed a similar pattern in other year groups.

Healthy conflict

Trust is necessary for colleagues to engage in open, constructive conflict. Conflict in this sense is not negative because it should be about concepts and ideas and is not personal. Trust enables colleagues to talk about the things that matter. Healthy conflict involves:

- Having lively, interesting meetings
- Extracting and exploiting the ideas of all team members
- Valuing dissenting views

Have lively, interesting meetings

Meetings can often feel frustrating for colleagues if they are not geared around important issues. For example, meetings where information is simply shared could easily be replaced with an email. Leaders need to make sure that meetings are meaningful, where critical topics are discussed to better understand them and solve problems.

> **Example**
>
> Matt is an assistant headteacher in charge of key stage 2. Recently, his meetings with the key stage 2 teachers have become somewhat stagnant. He has noticed a lack of energy in these meetings. After the last meeting, Matt asks the year 3 leader what she thinks. His colleague comments that it sometimes feels as if they meet for the sake of it rather than to do anything important. Matt discovers that this is a common feeling and decides to only meet when it is necessary to discuss something important. With the time saved, Matt commits to planning meetings more carefully to include some provocations to encourage more debate. The next meeting is scheduled to talk about assessment and data collection for the following term. Normally, Matt would simply clarify what testing is due and where to input the data. This time, he displays a statement on the board: We collect too much data. He asks year leaders to think for a minute and then to tell the team whether they agree or disagree with the statement, followed by an explanation. At the end of the meeting, the team agrees to drop a writing moderation exercise, as they feel that it is unnecessary at this time.

Extract and exploit the ideas of all team members

Meetings can sometimes be dominated by the loudest voices and if decisions are made based on only these, leaders would be making a mistake. They need to draw in everyone in order to achieve healthy conflict.

> **Example**
>
> Faiza is the headteacher of a small school. Many teachers have worked there for more than a decade but this year, the school has employed a new teacher, Carly. Carly is experienced and joins the school having relocated from another part of the country. In meetings, the established teachers dominate. They know the school and the community well and Carly doesn't seem to have a voice. Faiza knows all about Carly's expertise, having interviewed her at length. During a discussion on how pupil premium funding might be spent, the established teachers propose the same ideas that the school has done for the last few years. Faiza hears them out, then turns to Carly. 'Carly, we'd like to hear from you on this. I remember you telling me what a difference your initiative of vocabulary development made for disadvantaged children. Can you tell us about it?'

Value dissenting views

Harmony is, of course, desirable, but only when both the team and the children are performing well. Leaders need to be aware of artificial harmony, where there is the illusion of peace because colleagues are not saying what they think. If they value dissenting views, they can avoid working in an echo chamber where bad ideas could proliferate unchallenged.

> **Example**
>
> Aisha is the deputy headteacher of a large primary school and has a strong track record of improving the quality of teaching in maths. Aisha has a great reputation and is well liked by all colleagues because of her kindness and generosity. Aisha has identified an issue with fluency of number facts in Y1 and wants to introduce a programme designed to help children become fluent that could be used in class and at home. When Aisha pitches this to the team, they all smile and nod, indicating that they think it is a good idea. This has happened before and Aisha was uncomfortable with it then; she wants people to challenge such initiatives. The day before the meeting, she had been telling one of the Y1 teachers, Connie, about her problem. Connie admitted that it might be too much to add an initiative without taking something away and Aisha was pleased with the challenge. She asked Connie to say exactly that at the staff meeting and Connie obliges. After Connie airs her opinion, Aisha thanks Connie and tells the group how important it is to share dissenting opinions. A deeper discussion follows about what could be taken away to allow for Aisha's idea to happen.

Commitment

Conflict is necessary for colleagues to be able to commit. Sharing opinions comes before buying into decisions, and commitment is made up of:

- Creating clarity around direction and priorities
- Involving colleagues in decision-making
- Improving communication

Create clarity around direction and priorities

As we have seen in previous chapters, a clear strategic direction is necessary for leaders to communicate a clear purpose to colleagues. Research has shown that trust is positively related to continuous improvement efforts when employees strongly identified with the organisation[3].

> **Example**
>
> Elena is the new headteacher of a junior school. In her first month in the post, she examines the school's vision and values and has lots of conversations with lots of people about what the school is good at and what it needs to do better. She asks colleagues what makes them want to work here instead of the school down the road and what makes this school special. She begins to formulate the values that the colleagues, children and community share and puts this into words that everyone will understand. Elena shares these values with colleagues and tells stories of how they came about in order for every colleague to see themselves in the shared values. She identifies that there are several priorities all vying for attention, including improving behaviour, curriculum development, reducing a deficit budget and the teaching of early reading. When she presents these to colleagues, she explains that if everything is a priority, then nothing is. She asks each person to suggest the most pressing priority for the next term. Colleagues are unanimous in their choice – they feel that if behaviour was better, they would have the time to dedicate to the other priorities.

Involve colleagues in decision-making

If colleagues are going to buy into a decision, they need to have the opportunity to air their opinion. Not doing so risks apathy, at best, and frustrated defiance, at worst.

> **Example**
>
> Dinara is the year 5 leader in a three-form entry school. It is her responsibility to organise an upcoming trip to the local nature centre, but logistics mean that only half the year group can be accommodated at a time. Dinara has run this trip several times before but has a less experienced team. She knows exactly the kind of organisation needed to make it run smoothly. She also knows that such organisation means disruption to a normal day for teachers and teaching assistants, with different break times, different lunchtimes and mixed-up classes. Dinara is well aware that, in order for the trip to run smoothly, all colleagues need to have the opportunity to contribute to the plan. She calls a meeting with all teachers and TAs while the children are in assembly and presents the problem. She patiently asks what everyone thinks the best way of organising the trip would be, letting them come across the problems with break and lunch and resolving them without her input. With clarity over timings and who needs to be where, Dinara closes the meeting, content that everyone has had their say.

Improve communication

When trust is patchy or things are going wrong in a school, this often manifests as colleagues feeling as if they do not know what is going on. Decisions are sprung on them, perhaps because leaders are reactive to issues. Some know certain things while others do not. Hearsay rules. School leaders can always improve what and how they communicate and doing so builds trust.

> **Example**
>
> Penelope is the headteacher of an average-sized primary school. She has a small senior leadership team that work well together. They meet regularly and tend to solve problems quickly, often responding to new information and changing plans to address what they know. However, Penelope picks up that some colleagues feel out of the loop. This comes about after the timings for a music workshop are changed on the morning of the sessions and teachers did not know. Penelope realises that sometimes the SLT move so fast to diagnose and rectify problems that they neglect to communicate changes and the reasons for those changes in advance of them happening. Penelope makes a change. Now, at the end of every SLT meeting, she asks the same question of her team: what do we need to tell people and who will do it?

Holding to account

When colleagues are clear on what the collective goals are and have committed to action, leaders will need to considers ways of holding others to account for standards of performance and behaviour. Holding to account is often portrayed as having a difficult conversation, but that is the last stage, preceded by other activities that can help to reduce the need for those conversations:

- Openly publicise goals and standards
- Avoid excessive bureaucracy around performance management

Openly publicise goals and standards

Teachers have teacher standards and career stage expectations that they must meet, but these can sometimes be too detached from their day-to-day work and they may not be particularly inspiring. What leaders agree on as strategic priorities could become these publicly shared goals.

> **Example**
>
> Remember Elena, the new headteacher of a junior school. Elena and her colleagues agreed that behaviour was the most important priority for the coming term. Elena knows that simply saying their focus is on behaviour is not enough. She needs to set the standard of what teachers do that will improve behaviour. The SLT discuss and agree upon the key elements of managing behaviour well, including clarifying rules, teaching routines for entering the classroom, explaining clearly how children are expected to work on tasks and a signal for silence. The SLT take this to colleagues, acting on feedback received and refining their strategies. Elena then calls a staff meeting to explain the kind of behaviour she expects from children in the classroom, in the corridors and on the playground before explaining and modelling the strategies they have agreed to everyone.

Avoid excessive bureaucracy around performance management

Schools are notorious for excessive bureaucracy, particularly around performance evaluation. Written observation or book scrutiny feedback at untimely intervals are not designed to support improvement but to simply provide evidence of having checked. Simpler and more regular progress reviews might be more helpful – meaningful conversations that leave all parties in no doubt about what's going well and what needs to be better, including how that might be achieved.

> **Example**
>
> It is the beginning of a new academic year and Kate, the headteacher of an infant school, is considering appraisal targets for teachers. She is browsing the previous year's template and the feedback collected from an anonymous survey of teachers. She can see what they mean. The template is too long. There are far too many boxes to fill in with information that probably does not need recording. She decides to discuss with her SLT exactly what information actually needs to be recorded and what does not. The SLT strips back the template and Kate spends time checking this with HR and with the chair of governors to make sure that her pared down template stands up to scrutiny. When it is time to explain the changes to teachers, she is confident that they will need to spend less time on administrative issues and more time actually thinking about and acting on advice to improve.

Understanding your school culture and climate: building knowledge of self

It is very easy for leaders to have a blind spot when it comes to their own behaviours, particular around a virtue such as trustworthiness. Being such a positive attribute, it would be difficult for leaders to accept that they sometimes might not behave in a way that builds trust. They therefore need to spend time reflecting but also seek feedback to check the validity of their assumptions.

	Reflection prompt	**Seeking feedback**
Character	Think of a time when I did what I said I would do. Now think of a time when I didn't. Think of a time when I overpromised but underdelivered.	Tell me about a time when I did what I said I would do. Now tell me about a time when I didn't. Tell me about a time when my words and actions did not match.
Competence	Think of a time when I demonstrated that I could do the things I ask of others in a different role. Think of an example where I have not done this.	Tell me about a time when I walked the talk and did what I ask of others. Tell me about a time when I have not done this.
Vulnerability	Think of a time when I asked someone else for help. Think of a time when I admitted a mistake publicly out of choice. Think of a time when I asked for feedback on the way I handled a situation.	Tell me about a time when I asked you or someone else for help. Tell me about a time when I admitted a mistake publicly out of choice. Tell me about a time when I asked for feedback on the way I handled a situation.
Healthy conflict	Think of a meeting that I led recently that was lively and interesting. Now think of one that was boring and unnecessary. Think of a time when I sought out the views of all team members.	Tell me about a meeting that I led recently that was lively and interesting. Now tell me about one that was boring and unnecessary. Tell me about a time when I sought out the views of all team members.

	Reflection prompt	**Seeking feedback**
	Now think of a time when I did not.	Now tell me about a time when I did not.
	Think of a time when I actively encouraged dissenting opinions.	Tell me about a time when I actively encouraged dissenting opinions.
	Now think of a time when I just sought confirmation of what I thought.	Now tell me about a time when I appeared to be just seeking confirmation of what I thought.
Commitment	Think of a time when I clearly communicated our direction and priorities.	Tell me about a time when I clearly communicated our direction and priorities.
	Think of a time when I involved everyone in a decision.	Tell me about a time when I involved everyone in a decision.
	Now think of a time when I did not.	Now tell me about a time when I did not.
	Think of a time when I communicated a change clearly and in advance.	Tell me about a time when I communicated a change clearly and in advance.
	Now think of a time when I did not.	Now tell me about a time when I did not.
Holding to account	Think of a time when I openly publicised our goals or standards.	Tell me about a time when I openly publicised our goals or standards.
	Think of a time when I acted to avoid excessive bureaucracy.	Tell me about a time when I acted to avoid excessive bureaucracy.
	Now think of a time when I insisted on unnecessary bureaucracy.	Now tell me about a time when I insisted on unnecessary bureaucracy.

It is also useful to analyse when there were positive examples and when there were negative examples:

- Are all the positives with the same group of colleagues and all the negatives with a different group?
- Are the positives centred around a particular domain, such as curriculum development, while the negativities are centred around another, such as behaviour?

- Are there positive examples for just some of the elements of trust or across the board?
- What about for negative examples?

Understanding your school culture and climate: building knowledge of others

Leaders need to know the extent to which members of the team trust each other. This isn't easy to find out because truth does not always rise to the top. If there is an issue of mistrust within the team, those that feel it will need to have trust in someone in order to be comfortable sharing their concerns. Trust is also a very broad concept and, unless there is a shared understanding of what trust is, leaders are unlikely to find out useful information that can be acted on. It might be far more prudent to explore others' behaviours with the elements of trust in mind and the first method of doing so is through observation of how others interact.

Character

- Which colleagues do what they say they will do?
- Which colleagues overpromise but underdeliver?
- Which colleagues' words and actions match/don't match?

Competence

- Which teachers are capable of doing all the things they ask of their teaching assistants?
- Which teachers routinely demonstrate this?
- Which subject/year/phase leaders are capable of doing all the things they ask of teachers?
- Which middle leaders routinely demonstrate this?
- Which senior leaders are capable of doing all the things they ask of support staff/administration staff/teaching assistants/teachers/middle leaders?
- Which senior leaders routinely demonstrate this?

Vulnerability

- Which colleagues ask for help?
- Which colleagues readily admit when they have made a mistake?
- Which colleagues respond without defensiveness when asked about their work?
- Which colleagues proactively ask for feedback on their performance?

Healthy conflict

- Which meetings are lively and which are boring?
- Which middle/senior leaders seek out the views of all team members?
- Which middle/senior leaders actively encourage and reward dissenting opinions?

Commitment

- Which middle/senior leaders clearly communicate direction and priorities?
- Which middle/senior leaders involve their teams in decision-making?
- Which middle/senior leaders communicate clearly and in advance?

Holding to account

- Which middle/senior leaders openly publicise their team's/the school's goals and standards?
- Which middle/senior leaders avoid excessive bureaucracy?

The need for further exploration

Reflections on these observations might reveal situations that require more exploration. For example, if leaders noticed that there was a member of the senior leadership team that doesn't regularly do these things, a hypothesis might be that others could sometimes find them untrustworthy. Focusing in on what they do well along with what they do not do well can help to form useful feedback for that person. But leaders also need to realise that they'd be basing this on just their own opinion and that their perception may well be skewed. It would be inadvisable to ask colleagues about others directly but they could ask colleagues about leaders in general:

Character

- To what extent do leaders do what they say they will do?
- To what extent do leaders overpromise but underdeliver?
- To what extent do leaders' words and actions match?

Competence

- To what extent are leaders capable of doing all the things they ask of support staff/administration staff/teaching assistants/teachers/middle leaders?
- To what extent do leaders routinely demonstrate this?

Vulnerability

- To what extent do leaders ask for help?
- To what extent do leaders readily admit when they have made a mistake?
- To what extent do leaders respond without defensiveness when asked about their work?
- To what extent do leaders proactively ask for feedback on their performance?

Healthy conflict

- To what extent do leaders seek out the views of all team members?
- To what extent do leaders actively encourage and reward dissenting opinions?

Commitment

- To what extent do leaders clearly communicate direction and priorities?
- To what extent do leaders involve their teams in decision-making?
- To what extent do leaders communicate clearly and in advance?

Holding to account

- To what extent do leaders openly publicise their team's/the school's goals and standards?

- To what extent do leaders avoid excessive bureaucracy?

Pattern spotting

Either through conversation or survey, gathering the opinions of others can help leaders to develop a more rounded understanding of the collective perception of trustworthy behaviours. Aggregating this data can also provide information about particular behaviours that are stronger or lacking:

- Do some colleagues appear to have more trust in some leaders than others?
- Does there appear to be less trust associated with certain domains, such as assessment or SEND provision?

Using knowledge of trust for self-improvement

Reflecting on these prompts and gathering information about ourselves and others can yield a huge amount of information that could be incredibly useful. Ironically, for talking about trust, the importance of acting on information gathered is paramount. Leaders must accept uncomfortable feedback and work to act on it just as much as they celebrate positive feedback.

> **Example**
>
> Maryam is a year 4 leader in a primary school and her team, including teachers and teaching assistants, is quite large. Through conversations, Maryam realises that she rarely asks for help or feedback on how she leads. She plans to bring this up in a team meeting. She opens the meeting by making herself vulnerable: 'Thanks for coming everyone. The reason for us getting together is because I want to improve as a leader and to do that, I need your help. I see my job as keeping us focussed on the right things and supporting us all to be able to do that, free from anything that might waste our time. But I'm keen to know how I'm doing. With those things in mind, I'd like you to tell me three things using a simple start, stop, continue framework: What should I start doing? What should I stop doing? What should I continue doing?' Maryam knows that this kind of conversation is out of the ordinary and that others might not at first be prepared to give anything other than positive feedback. To help with momentum, she spoke to one of the teachers and one of the teaching assistants in her team a couple of days before the meeting, asking them to think about and contribute during the meeting. Their initial contributions make others more comfortable in sharing their feedback.

Using knowledge of trust to support others to improve

Sharing information helps to develop a collective understanding of the culture that is the result of (and contributes to) the level of trust in the school. If other leaders know the extent of the important behaviours, they are better placed to influence each other to behave in ways that could positively affect trust.

> **Example**
>
> Osmaan is the headteacher of a primary school. He asks his senior leadership team (a deputy headteacher and an assistant headteacher) to explore with those they line manage the extent to which the leadership team demonstrates trusting behaviours and to be ready to discuss their findings. The deputy headteacher goes first: 'People seem happy with the leadership team in terms of character – the feedback is that if we say we're going to do something we do it. But people found it harder to talk about the prompts in the commitment section. The general perception is that we don't communicate our priorities or involve people in deciding what they are'. Osmaan is keen to know whether this is the experience of others too and asks the assistant head what she thinks.
>
> 'I have similar feedback to share and it made me think: What are our priorities at the moment? I don't think I could explain that confidently if I needed to. I know we need to improve reading results and that we need to be doing more for children eligible for pupil premium. And the art curriculum needs to be reviewed, plus the early identification of SEND in year 1. But that's a lot'.
>
> Osmaan agrees and reminds the team that if everything is a priority, then nothing is. Osmaan then leads a brief discussion about what the priorities are at the moment and sketches out with the team how they will involve others in deciding the priorities. He knows that colleagues need to weigh in if they are to buy in and sets up a staff meeting to clarify direction.

Amplify anecdotes to drive others' behaviour

> **Example**
>
> Safah, a key stage 1 phase leader, wants to encourage others to speak up more with dissenting views. In the next team meeting, she makes a point of telling a story about her teaching assistant. Earlier that week, Safah and her teaching assistant had been discussing which children needed some additional support and how they might provide it. Safah had asked the teaching assistant to take two children during assembly to reinforce some

> number bonds to 10. The teaching assistant challenged the idea, reminding Safah that these two children had already missed several assemblies this term and that they often end up going to break a little late, which might well have worse consequences on their motivation than any benefit they might gain from the additional work. Safah and her teaching assistant then continued the discussion to find alternative times to fit the intervention work in.

Chapter summary

- Trust is not just nice to have but is a prerequisite for student achievement.
- Trust is built over many seemingly insignificant interactions.
- Trust cannot be built in isolation from the core business of improving schools – they are inextricably linked.
- Trust is a function of:
    - character
    - competence
    - vulnerability
    - healthy conflict
    - commitment
    - holding to account
- Vulnerability involves:
    - admitting weaknesses and mistakes
    - accepting questions and input about areas of responsibility
- Healthy conflict involves:
    - having lively, interesting meetings
    - extracting and exploiting the ideas of all team members
    - valuing dissenting views
- Commitment involves:
    - creating clarity around direction and priorities

- involving colleagues in decision-making
- improving communication
■ Holding to account involves:
  - openly publicising goals and standards
  - avoiding excessive bureaucracy around performance management

References

1. Lencioni, P. (2013). *The five dysfunctions of a team*. San Francisco, Calif.: Jossey-Bass.
2. Bryk, A., & Schneider, B. (2004). *Trust in schools*. New York: Russell Sage Foundation.
3. Robinson, V. (2017). 'Capabilities required for leading improvement: Challenges for researchers and developers'. Research conference. https://research.acer.edu.au/cgi/viewcontent.cgi?article=1306&context=research_conference.
4. Covey, S., & Merrill, R. (2017). *The speed of trust*. New York, NY: Free Press.
5. Feltman, C. (2009). *The thin book of trust*. Oregon: Thin Book Publishing.
6. Gottman, J. (2011). *The science of trust*. New York: W.W. Norton.
7. Hoy, Wayne, & Tschannen-Moran, Megan. (1999). 'Five faces of trust: an empirical confirmation in urban elementary schools'. *Journal of School Leadership*, 9, 184–208. DOI: 10.1177/105268469900900301
8. Artz, Benjamin, Goodall, Amanda H., & Oswald, Andrew J. (2014). 'Boss competence and worker well-being'. Available at SSRN: https://ssrn.com/abstract=2514752 or http://dx.doi.org/10.2139/ssrn.2514752.

Part 3
How do leaders go about culture change?

Part 3 preamble

Culture change

Introduction

Whether you're a new leader or an established one, the chances are that you'll need to tackle a variety of problems and the culture that exists in your school will either help or hinder those efforts. In order to bring about improvements, leaders need to learn to influence their team's underlying beliefs and assumptions. In Part 3, the contextual differences between influencing culture as a new and as an established leader are identified and the book ends with a discussion around the extent to which culture and climate can be measured.

What is culture influenced by?

While Part 2 of this book described and exemplified some of the elements of culture and climate, Part 3 is concerned with the process of how culture and climate might be changed.

Edgar Schein offers three fundamental influencers of culture[1]:

- The founder's beliefs, values and assumptions
- The learning experiences of colleagues as the school develops
- New beliefs, values and assumptions introduced by new leaders or colleagues

Two common scenarios

It is rare for schools to be in the position of the first situation (starting a new school from scratch), so Part 3 of this book takes a closer look at two common scenarios related to Schein's cultural influencers:

- A new leader in a school (whether internally promoted or new to the school)
- An established leader in a school who wants to make a change

Choosing the right goal

Whether a new or established leader, it is quite likely that there will be differences between their underling beliefs and assumptions and those that are already part of the school culture and it can be tempting to formulate the goal of 'changing the culture'. This, however, should not be the goal for two reasons. The first is that, as Viviane Robinson advises[1], leaders should not design the future until they deeply understand the present. The second is that a goal of 'changing the culture' is just not specific enough. The model of marginal gains, popularised by former British cycling coach Sir Dave Brailsford, advocates small but significant changes that can lead to monumental results.

School leaders need to consider what problem needs to be solved. There is an important reason for this. A leader might impose new ways of working, but these efforts will not result in culture change unless they lead to recognisable success that the team attributes to these new ways of working. This is fundamental to the mantra of *improvement rather than change*. Leaders also have a decision to make about whether they adopt a surplus model for improvement – where they seek to build on known strengths to solve a problem – or a deficit model – where they seek to correct perceived weaknesses to bring about improvement. In addition, leaders ought to be clear about their ultimate goal, but, understanding the importance of autonomy, they must also allow for flexibility for how that goal might be achieved.

Both scenarios require time and unlearning

There are several features in common between the two scenarios that leaders need to be aware of. The first is that changing deeply embedded assumptions takes time and effort. The second is that leaders need to plan for unlearning as well as introducing something new. Dropping some practices is necessary to create time and to give new ways of thinking and working the best chance of becoming embedded.

Both scenarios require the prioritisation of psychological safety

Psychological safety was a theme throughout Part 2 and Schein has this to add about how it is achieved:

- Present a compelling positive vision – we'll be better if we learn the new way of thinking/working
- Provide formal training in the new way of thinking/working
- Involve people in how to access informal training
- Create space and time to practice – give time, resources, coaching and feedback
- Provide positive role models so that colleagues can see what 'it' looks like
- Create support groups where problems can be discussed

Both scenarios benefit from multiple mechanisms working in harmony

Schein also identified primary and secondary mechanisms for changing cultures – tools that leaders have at their disposal to influence the way that their team thinks, feels and behaves. The primary mechanisms are easier for leaders to control because they represent their own behaviours, but the secondary mechanisms are harder to control and involve the interaction of colleagues going about their work. The important point to note, as you'll see in the following chapters, is that the mechanisms must consistently and simultaneously convey the same message, leaving no room for ambiguity.

Primary mechanisms

- What school leaders pay attention to
- How school leaders react to critical incidents
- How leaders allocate resources
- Deliberate role modelling, teaching and coaching
- How leaders allocate rewards and status
- Recruitment, promotion and performance management

Secondary mechanisms

- Organisational design and structure
- Organisational systems and procedures
- Design of physical space and buildings
- Stories and myths about key people and events
- Formal mission statements, charters and ethical code

Reference

1. Schein, E. (1986). *Organizational culture and leadership.* San Francisco, CA: Jossey-Bass.

 Influencing culture as a new leader

Introduction

You might have just taken on your first middle leadership role or been promoted into senior leadership. You might be taking on your first headship or taking on another headship in a different school. Being a new leader brings with it both challenges and opportunities to influence the culture and this chapter looks in detail at what those challenges and opportunities are. It explains the mechanisms that leaders can use to bring about improvement and provides examples of each so that new leaders are equipped to teach their schools how to think, feel and behave.

New leader dynamics

Taking up a leadership position in a school, whether an internal promotion or at a completely new school, is daunting. All eyes and ears pick up everything done and said, with each analysed in detail. There will be an undercurrent of apprehension. A new leader can be seen as a threat to established ways of working that provides colleagues with security, familiarity and therefore safety. A new leader has a gloriously complex problem of bringing about improvement while navigating these individual and collective thoughts and emotions. But the context brings with it an opportunity.

Schein describes a three-part process for a new leader's (ideal) pattern of influence:

- Compliance
- Success
- Shared values

The first stage is compliance. The new leader might impose ways of working early on in their tenure that colleagues comply with simply because they have come from the new boss. Many colleagues will be seeking to build a relationship with the new leader, to figure out (or influence) their place in the new pecking order, so the new leader can expect some form of compliance early on with any proposed new ways of working. Compliance is an ugly word, though. It implies reluctance. Consider these two examples:

> **Example A**
>
> Sara is the new headteacher and she has decided that, from the outset, she wants to focus on behaviour. She has strategies that she knows well and that brought success in her last school. On the very first INSET day, she takes some time to set out her ideas for tackling low level disruption, providing opportunities for discussion so that she can check colleagues' understanding of what she is advocating. Over the next few days and weeks, Sara is relentless in walking the school, coaching colleagues in managing situations and reinforcing her strategies. 'Finally, we're doing something about behaviour! I can see an improvement already', comments one colleague to another after a few days. This seems to be a sentiment that is felt across the majority of the school.

> **Example B**
>
> Sam is the new headteacher and he has decided that he wants to bring in a maths scheme that he knows very well and which brought success in his last school. On the very first INSET day, he takes some time to set out how the maths scheme works and provides opportunities for discussion so that he can check colleagues' understanding of what he is advocating. Over the next few days and weeks, Sam is relentless in walking the school, coaching colleagues in teaching using the scheme and reinforcing his strategies. 'It seems a bit unnecessary to have changed. It's just like our old scheme', comments one colleague to another after a few days. This seems to be a sentiment that is felt across the majority of the school.

In both examples, the new headteacher introduces an initiative that has worked for them in a previous school. In both examples, the headteacher has brought about a quick change in how something works – behaviour in Example A and maths in Example B. Sara, in Example A, has been fortunate. What she believes to be important in leading a school (focusing on behaviour) is what that school needed. However, what Sam believes to be important in leading a school (maths) was probably not a priority.

This brings us to the second stage of Schein's process of a new leader's pattern of influence – success. In Example A, there seems to be an element of success in what Sara has done. Colleagues are seeing her strategies working and this will reinforce the idea that what they are now doing about behaviour is the right thing to do. On the other hand, in Example B, Sam's colleagues are not so positive. They have not seen that what they are doing is improving things and they are beginning to question the decision to change at all. Sara has influenced success while Sam has not.

The third stage of Schein's process for a new leader's pattern of influence is shared values. In Example A, the success that Sara's colleagues have experienced has resulted in them sharing a positive experience and, as a result, the team has adopted Sara's beliefs and assumptions about how to manage behaviour – she has instigated a cultural change where there is now broad agreement amongst the team (and with her) about what works in managing behaviour. But in Example B, there is no such shared experience. The team might be persisting (for a while) with the maths scheme that Sam has brought in but, because there has been no success, Sam hasn't managed to align his colleagues' beliefs and assumptions.

Sara was fortunate in that her assumptions about what leaders should do aligned with what the school needed while Sam's did not. To simplify the examples (and make the point about the need for success in order for initial compliance to result in a culture change), neither leader took time to do one thing that may have improved their early leadership – understanding the present.

Understand the present

Each chapter in Part 2 invited the reader to develop hidden knowledge of their own school in relation to:

- Building psychological safety, sharing vulnerability and establishing purpose
- Leaders' expectations and biases
- Autonomy, mastery and purpose as the drivers for motivation
- Relational trust

It is this process that will help a new leader to deeply understand the present – a prerequisite for making the right choice of goal. Sara in Example A would have realised the need for work on behaviour and this could have helped her in implementing her behaviour strategy. Sam in Example B would have realised that maths probably didn't need so much attention or, if it did, he may have realised that transplanting a whole scheme was not what was actually needed. Both leaders in these examples bypassed colleagues' theories of action (the underlying beliefs that sustain their actions):

> To make improvement more likely and to avoid the consequences that Sam will have to deal with in Example B, a new leader needs to quickly figure out what problems need to be solved through inviting honest and upward feedback and engaging with colleagues' theories of action.

Choose the right problem to focus on

Remember, despite the importance of school culture, trying to change it directly is futile. Culture change needs to happen through addressing education-specific problems to have meaning because collective actions and beliefs (culture) will be influencing the problem as it manifests.

Viviane Robinson suggests a four-part process for engaging with colleagues' theories of action:

- Agree on the problem to be solved
- Inquire into the relevant theory of action
- Evaluate the relative merit of the current and alternative theories of action
- Implement and monitor a new, sufficiently shared theory of action

Example C

Nila is the new headteacher and she has spent some time getting to know the school before her start date. She has looked at available data on the school website, read the latest Ofsted report and checked out financial benchmarking data in the public domain. On top of this, she has had lengthy conversations with the chair of governors and her soon-to-be leadership team about what they think the school needs to do to improve. From all this information, Nila has a hunch that the teaching of reading is an area that needs to be improved. Nila addresses colleagues on the first INSET day: 'Thank you for making me feel so welcome. I am really excited to be here and part of the team. I appreciate how difficult it can be to have a new headteacher and I want to reassure you of a couple of things. I am not here to make changes for change's sake. You will not hear me talking about what I did in my previous school and you will certainly not have to put up with me trying to make our school like my last one. We are unique. We have our own ways of working, our own strengths and our own problems to solve. And this is what I will be focusing on in the next few weeks. I need to get to know how we work inside and out in order to make good decisions. I'll be asking you all lots of questions but that is only so that I can understand. These conversations will often start with me asking about what we're good at and what you think we could be better at...'

Over the next few weeks, Nila explores her hunch about the teaching of reading needing to improve. She finds that, in the early years and in year 1, there is a strong emphasis on phonics. When children move up into older year groups, though, the systematic teaching of phonics seems to develop into a simple model of comprehension practice where children read a text and answer questions about it. She speaks to some teachers who routinely teach in this way and discovers that they have always done it like that. More importantly, she uncovers the belief that, because of SATs being structured in this way, this is how to prepare children for the tests.

She speaks to a couple of teachers and teaching assistants that have recently moved from year 1 to year 3 and are frustrated by the lack of structure in reading lessons compared to the phonics programme used in the infant years. She also speaks to the reading leader (one of the teachers in year 5) who seems to do more than the comprehension tasks. Discussion with that teacher reveals that she is also dissatisfied and has been experimenting with strategies that she has read about in books and blog posts.

Nila meets with teachers after the first few weeks and poses a question for colleagues to discuss – what makes great teaching of reading? The team collects a number of different ideas and Nila encourages everyone to have a voice. She explains that it seems like reading might be a good area to focus on, particularly the teaching of reading beyond phonics. She realises that this might not directly involve all colleagues, mainly those teaching year 2 to year 6, and reassures them that their opinions are important, but, if they feel their presence is unnecessary at any point, to bring it up with her. Nila adds that she has some experience in this area and talks about the kind of things she believes to be important in the teaching of reading, giving examples such as teaching background knowledge and vocabulary and emphasising fluency and prosody. Perhaps most importantly, she explains her belief that teaching reading is about more than just preparing children for a test and that, even though results could be better, there are other ways to prepare them while making sure that children enjoy reading and experience some of the greatest books ever written. She asks the team whether anyone is already doing any of these things. In the discussion that follows, it appears that elements of Nila's suggestions are dotted around the key stage 2 teachers. Not wanting to overload her colleagues, she starts to draw the meeting to a close but ends by asking for volunteers to be part of a smaller team that will drive this work.

In this example, Nila:

- Agrees with the team on the problem to be solved (improving the teaching of reading beyond phonics)
- Inquires into the relevant theories of action (for both those that were setting comprehension tasks and those that were doing other things)
- Involves the team in evaluating the relative merit of the current and alternative theories of action

Design the future

With a clear understanding of the present, the next stage is to design the future. It can be tempting to start with describing culture in terms that are too vague, such as wanting everyone to feel psychologically safe, or for everyone to feel autonomy and flow, or for everyone to have high levels of trust, but remember that these are the results of school culture – the climate that exists because of how everyone behaves. They are desirable, but not helpful, in mapping out how to achieve them.

It can also be tempting to start with describing some generic ways of behaving, such as wanting everyone to share their vulnerabilities or for leaders to notice their biases or communicate a clear purpose. Again, these are desirable but cannot be divorced from the process of solving problems. To help colleagues to modify behaviours, desirable behaviours need to be concrete, exemplified in the tackling of a problem.

So, leaders might then start to list the specific behaviours that are required to tackle the given problem. In our example, the problem is the teaching of reading beyond phonics.

> **Example C (continued)**
>
> Nila meets with the volunteer team (the early adopters) and sets about clarifying what it is that teachers might do. They come up with a list:
>
> - Teach the meaning of important words that come up in the text
> - Teach background knowledge that children will need to understand the text
> - Focus on fluency (children will not be able to understand if they do not read fluently with expression)
> - Set a variety of comprehension tasks that check for understanding (not just 'read and answer questions')

This discussion is vital. Not only do the early adopters agree on the kinds of things that teachers might do to teach reading, the discussion itself firms up the shared beliefs that the group has and will aim to influence others to have. The discussion would also need to take into account concepts from Part 2 of this book. For example, leaders will need to look for opportunities for autonomy over, to name just a few variables, text choice, how to explain and reinforce the meaning of vocabulary and which comprehension tasks to use with a given text.

Prioritise aligning beliefs and values

Sara and Sam, the headteachers in Examples A and B earlier in this chapter, both chose a model for getting colleagues to believe in new ways of thinking (though only Sara was successful). Both would have benefitted from taking more time to align colleagues' beliefs and values. This is much more than a moment standing in front of colleagues and it is much more than the examples given so far in this chapter. It is done daily, through all sorts of interactions with different colleagues:

- Keep talking about beliefs and assumptions – ask what others think and tell others what you think, looking for common ground.
- Get to know individuals' beliefs and assumptions – build up a picture of what each person values and what drives their behaviour.
- Notice language that contradicts your beliefs and assumptions – challenge its use and provide alternatives.
- Notice practices that contradict your beliefs and assumptions – ask why these practices exist and point out that they contradict your beliefs.

The importance of aligning beliefs and values cannot be underestimated for a new leader. Doing so provides the foundation for good implementation. It can't be rushed.

Example C (continued)

Nila develops a system in school to support teachers during their PPA time. Each team has PPA time together so that they can have fruitful discussions and every two weeks, because it is a priority, she or the reading leader joins each key stage 2 team for part of the session to collaborate on planning reading lessons. Nila meets with the year 4 team and lets the team carry out their meeting, just listening at first. The team discuss the upcoming sequence of lessons and agree on four lessons for the following week. Nila is pleased with how the conversation goes and has nothing to add. Then the conversation turns to what they will teach on the fifth day next week. One teacher suggests that they do a comprehension and pulls up a file that they used the previous year – a text and a page of questions. Nila does not say anything at first, waiting to see if anyone will challenge this idea. The team seems to accept it even though it doesn't fit with the quality of the sequence planned for the first four days. Nila steps in: 'You've planned such a good sequence for the first part of the week, which includes the ideas that we have been talking about recently including teaching vocabulary and background knowledge to understand the text that you've focused on. It feels as if the plan for day 5 does not meet that standard. Tell me again the reason for doing it?'

The discussion reveals a misconception that a sequence of learning needs to be a week long and the teachers were looking to fill a day so that the next sequence could start afresh the week after. One of the teachers challenges this, though, questioning why sequences of lessons need to be like that. She suggests two options. The first is to think

> of an additional comprehension task that could reinforce children's understanding of the text studied for the first four days and the second is to start the next sequence earlier. The team discusses the options and Nila is content that whatever option they choose will work.

Prioritise psychological safety

The new leader must understand that the process of aligning beliefs and values, particularly when it comes to challenging or questioning underlying assumptions, will likely create anxiety and defensiveness. Everyone needs stability but, to bring about educational improvement, this sort of challenging and questioning is necessary. The way that it is done makes a significant difference to the climate, though. Chapter 4 described some of the strategies for building safety, summarised here:

- Show warmth and kindness in every interaction
- Give good eye contact
- Engage in frequent, energetic exchanges
- Close physical proximity (but not too close)
- Prevent interruptions
- Eat together
- Encourage humour and laughter
- Treat individuals as unique and valued
- Give small attentive courtesies
- Show that you care
- Make mixing happen
- Ask questions to draw others out
- Celebrate the humblest of tasks
- Narrate others' role in the future
- Create connections between people

Closely related to psychological safety is the importance of leaders sharing their vulnerability. Chapter 4 described some of the strategies for sharing vulnerability, summarised here:

- Seek feedback
- Face uncomfortable truths head on
- Debrief decision-making

Schein's work on organisational culture also outlines strategies to build psychological safety and has these to add:

Strategy	Example
Present a compelling positive vision – we'll be better if we learn the new way of thinking/working	Nila talks excitedly about the difference that she expects their work on reading beyond phonics to make, particularly for the least advantaged children. She uses stories from the early adopters to draw attention to how enjoyable it is to teach children when they are being successful and how it only takes a small number of minor tweaks to a sequence of learning to make it happen.
Provide formal training in the new way of thinking/working	Nila and the reading leader set up short training sessions to address each active ingredient of their emerging reading strategy. They provide reasons why explicitly teaching vocabulary is important and show multiple examples of how teachers might choose to do it. They do the same thing with a session on developing reading fluency, explaining the rationale for working on it alongside modelling some strategies for teachers to use, such as repeated re-reading with emphasis on different words to see how it changes the meaning of the sentence and marking up a text for expression.
Involve people in how to access informal training	Nila knows that the formal training will not be enough to bring about improvement. She knows that teachers are going to need to experience success using these strategies for them to become embedded (indeed that she should only work towards embedding them if they bring about success). This means creating more opportunities for colleagues to engage with the assumptions and behaviours related to the emerging reading strategy. She and the reading leader encourage colleagues to watch each other and use the shared experience for conversations about reading. The reading leader makes sure that each colleague has the opportunity to do so and Sam is keen for colleagues to have autonomy over who they work with.

Strategy	Example
	Nila also collates a list of books, blog posts and podcasts about reading that she can use when a need naturally arises in conversation. Commonly, during conversations about reading, she is able to add: 'I know a great blog post that explores exactly that issue – it is about a nine-minute read. I'll forward it to you…'
Create space and time to practice – give time, resources, coaching and feedback	Nila resists the urge to observe lessons. She knows that she can learn enough about how the implementation of the reading strategy is going through conversations aggregated from the experiences of different leaders. Nila keeps asking: 'What do you need that you don't already have that will help with teaching reading?' Two things come up. The first is more and better books – whole class sets. The second is some additional time to watch others and to discuss reading planning.
Create support groups where problems can be discussed	Nila knows that colleagues will come across difficulties and wants to create a forum where problem solving can be collaborative. She arranges for a fortnightly meeting where all those who are planning reading can meet with the reading leader in a surgery style. They can bring any issues, find out if and how others have approached them and support each other to adapt what they are doing. One common theme is supporting children who have not yet got sufficient phonological awareness and still need some intervention. If they missed reading lessons for this, then they would fall further behind with comprehension. The team decide to trial short phonics interventions for 20 minutes before school so that they can still take part in the reading lessons with the rest of the class.

Teach your school how to perceive, think, feel and behave

Schein described tools that leaders can use to teach their organisations to perceive, think, feel and behave. A new leader will have to carefully manage the first six (what Schein calls the primary mechanism), carrying them all out simultaneously and ensuring consistency of message.

What to pay attention to

The things that leaders notice and comment on become the things that others think leaders value and they will often adjust their behaviour accordingly. Leaders' attention is also revealed through what they decide to measure, control or reward.

The implication for leaders is that they must be deliberate and systematic in what they pay attention to in order to influence the behaviours of others. In the examples above, Nila systematically pays attention to reading in a number of different ways in lots of different interactions, clearly communicating what she believes to be important. A common mistake is for leaders to launch an initiative and then not systematically follow it up with appropriate attention. Nila could have declared victory too soon after the early work on defining a reading strategy and spent more of her time on finance, risk assessments or behaviour. She will undoubtedly have had to pay attention to those things, but the key point is that she did not let them distract her from her continued attention to reading, for she knew that if her attention appeared to wane, then so would her colleagues'. Not paying sustained attention to priorities creates a vacuum where colleagues will spend time and energy trying to figure out what leaders want and this risks the creation of multiple subcultures where different groups do different things because of the different inferences they have made. A lack of consistency here prevents the primary mechanisms from reinforcing each other.

This can also be exacerbated by paying attention to too many things – if everything is important, then nothing is. Leaders must therefore be careful about what to not pay attention to. This can be equally powerful in reinforcing key messages.

Example C (continued)

Throughout the development stage of the reading strategy beyond phonics, Nila deliberately does not bring up marking because she wants to make sure that colleagues don't perceive this to be something of importance. She is prepared to address it when it comes up, though, because she knows that the existing culture is for teachers to spend hours marking children's comprehension work for what seems like no benefit. The question comes up after a week or so – one teacher wants to know how they should mark the work that children produce in books on vocabulary. The next time the team meets together, she brings it up: 'I've had a question about marking and I have quite strong opinions on it. I know how long we used to spend on marking and I know that I'm asking you to spend more time on planning reading. Therefore, something has to give and it has to be marking. I'm not saying don't look at the work that children produce but I am saying that there are better, more efficient ways to check that children have understood and to give timely and useful feedback. All I want us to focus on for the time being is the active ingredients that we have agreed and getting into the habit of planning improved sequences of learning'. Whenever Nila is in a classroom, whenever she is looking at children's books, she deliberately never brings up how work is marked, only discussing the extent to which children have understood the vocabulary, the background knowledge and the texts.

How to react to critical incidents

A critical incident is anything that is perceived to be critical. For a new leader this might be, for example:

- An Ofsted inspection
- An incident leading to an exclusion
- A resignation
- Poor performance on statutory assessment
- An outbreak of illness
- A necessary school closure

Of course, the early stages of a new leader probably count as a critical incident and the important thing for leaders to understand and act on is the likely increase in anxiety that many colleagues will experience. The main priority when reacting to critical incidents must be psychological safety.

How to allocate resources

The way that leaders allocate resources demonstrates what they value. These might be physical resources or they might be how people are deployed.

> **Example C (continued)**
>
> Nila, the new headteacher prioritising reading beyond phonics, knows the power of cultural artifacts in influencing what colleagues do. Part of the strategy development is to review the reading spine – the books that children will read throughout key stage 2 as part of reading lessons. A lot of time and research goes into selecting these books and colleagues are involved in the decisions. Nila decides to allocate several thousand pounds, supplemented by some PTA funding, to purchase class sets of key texts. She also makes sure that either she or the reading leader are available fortnightly to support teachers during PPA with planning reading sequences.

Deliberate role modelling, teaching and coaching

The leader is the main role model for the school, year groups or phase. Everything that leaders do – from what they pay attention to to the energy and interactions that they have – has a strong influence on culture.

> **Example C (continued)**
>
> Nila knows that she needs credibility in the eyes of her new colleagues. She knows that she is asking her team to take risks in trying new ways of working and she needs to show that she is up to that challenge too. She wants to create a culture where colleagues ask for feedback and are comfortable having others in the room while they teach as a source of feedback. By arranging with each teacher in advance, she and the reading leader teach each class and seek feedback from each teacher about what worked well and what could have been better.

How to allocate rewards and status

Rewards available to the new leader are, first and foremost, the interactions that they have. It can mean a lot to colleagues who may be feeling some anxiety about the change in leadership to have their opinions sought and their practice championed. With this comes status.

> **Example**
>
> During her regular conversations and walks of the school, Nila finds a bright spot in year 3, where children talk particularly enthusiastically about the books they are studying. They use key vocabulary accurately in context and the teacher (Zak) seems to have developed some very effective ways of managing class discussions to develop their understanding. Nila decides to spotlight this success in a number of ways. First, she directs other colleagues to talk to Zak and to arrange to see him teaching. Then, during a training session where the team is reviewing strategies for teaching reading, Nila asks Zak to talk through an example of how he manages group discussions. At the end, Nila once again encourages others to chat to Zak and arrange to see what he does in action.

Recruitment, promotion and performance management

The team that leaders assemble has the potential to reinforce school culture. There is a balance that leaders should try to achieve here, though. While it may be useful to have a team that shares beliefs, values and assumptions, it is also important to encourage alternative points of view to avoid creating an echo chamber.

> **Example C (continued)**
>
> During her first term as headteacher, Nila (who has been working on developing a reading strategy) receives a resignation from a teacher who is relocating and needs to recruit a replacement for January. When she shows potential candidates around, she talks about their priority of reading and introduces them to key people such as Zak from the previous example and the reading leader, encouraging them to talk about reading. The interview process includes teaching a reading lesson and some of the questions are designed to find out what the candidates' underlying assumptions about reading are in order to see the extent of a match between each candidate and the emerging culture. Nila also creates opportunities on the interview day for other colleagues to get to know the candidates because she knows that the more people she can get opinions from about which candidate is the best fit, the more valid her decision will be. This also helps to build trust with her team, as she is asking their opinion on an important matter such as recruitment.

The secondary mechanisms

The secondary mechanisms are developed over time and are explained in more detail in the context of an existing leader aiming to influence culture in the next chapter. For reference, the secondary mechanisms are:

- Organisational design and structure
- School systems and procedures
- Rites and rituals of the school
- Design of physical space
- Stories and myths about key people and events
- Formal mission statements, charters and ethical code

Chapter summary

- The new-to-the-school or new-to-the-role leader might impose ways of working fairly soon into their leadership that colleagues comply with simply because they have come from a new authority figure.
- For the new ways of working to stick, colleagues need to experience success and, importantly, attribute that success to the new way of working.

- If this happens, the group will develop genuine shared values and induct new members into the group according to those values.
- New leaders need to take time to understand the present by inquiring into the culture and climate of the school.
- But this cannot be done generally. This knowledge building needs to be based around specific problems. Doing so will help the new leader to choose the right problem to focus on.
- New leaders need to design the future with the team – to set the strategic direction so that colleagues understand where they're going and why.
- New leaders ought to prioritise aligning colleagues' beliefs and values.
- Psychological safety will always be at risk when there is a change of leadership, so new leaders must understand and prioritise it.
- What new leaders pay attention to and how they allocate resources clearly communicates to colleagues what is important, so think it through carefully.

Influencing culture as an established leader

Introduction

You might have been in your school for a number of years as a middle leader, a senior leader or the headteacher. Being an established leader brings with it different challenges and opportunities to those experienced by new leaders and, because of the likelihood of having a well-defined culture (whether that is deliberate or not), there will be times when established leaders need to make changes to seek improvement. This chapter looks in detail at what those challenges and opportunities are and explains the mechanisms that leaders can use to bring about improvement, providing examples of each so that established leaders are equipped to teach their schools how to think, feel and behave in new ways.

Established leader dynamics

It is not uncommon for established leaders to come to the conclusion that they need to push the reset button and this presents different challenges to those faced as a new leader. The new leader has the opportunity to create change in the pursuit of improvement purely because of their appointment (it is expected among colleagues that there will be changes). But the established leader will have already embedded (by design or by chance) a culture in their school that is inextricably linked to them as a leader and they will have deeply embedded relationships with colleagues, both of which will provide some level of predictability, stability and safety.

A school with established leadership is likely to have developed various subgroups that will probably have developed their own variations of the school culture. Successful schools may well have shifted from one leader influencing much of the culture to the emergence of multiple leaders in different key stages or subjects, each doing a great job with their teams. Schein talks about these kind of organisations as 'midlife'. There might be a strong culture and a positive climate but, if there is not, the established leader faces a specific challenge of the established culture protecting what has worked in the past rather than supporting the solving of current problems.

Create a motivation for change

Schein describes a three-part process for a midlife organisation to bring about improvement and the first stage is to create the motivation for change. This might result from external pressure – in schools, probably the most common form is an Ofsted inspection where areas for improvement are reported. However, there are other possible triggers that an established leader might use to motivate change, including:

- A change in DfE statutory responsibilities (such as the revised EYFS framework)
- A change to statutory assessment (such as the introduction of the phonics screening and multiplication tables check, or the removal of SATs at key stage 1)
- A period of staff turnover
- A significant change to the leadership team

The important element of this motivation for change is that the established leader needs to enable colleagues to see that a change is necessary.

> **Example**
>
> Helen has been the headteacher for several years and has a well-established team. Over the last few years, the number on roll has been steadily dropping due to a dip in the local birth rate. The school has always run on the model of having one teaching assistant per class, but this is less financially viable as each year comes and, when two teaching assistants retire in the summer, Helen knows that she is not in a position to be able to afford to replace them like for like and that her leadership team must consider a different model for classroom support. The teachers are very much used to having a teaching assistant with them and Helen predicts that the necessary change will be unsettling.
>
> Helen thinks carefully about how to bring the subject up with the teaching team. She knows that the necessary change in culture needs to be tied to a goal and that she needs to manage the anxiety by prioritising psychological safety. She meets with the leadership team first to firm up the problem so that she can communicate it in a way that will motivate the necessary changes. The leadership team comes up with two goals:
>
> - Responsible budget planning that does not result in a deficit
> - Ensuring the right support for children in the classroom

Aligning beliefs and assumptions

The second stage of Schein's model for the established leader to bring about improvement is the alignment of beliefs and assumptions. In a midlife organisation such as Helen's school, there are likely to be subcultures in different key stages that work very well, so what is important for a leader in Helen's position is to ensure there is absolute clarity of goal and of how each team talks about it.

> **Example**
>
> Helen knows that her teaching team work with the underlying assumption and belief that each class has a teaching assistant, but this model is financially unviable. She also knows that the teaching assistants find great security in having a classroom base and the predictability of working with the same children and teacher for the year. She meets with her leadership team to talk through how this needs to be modified in order for the necessary changes to be successful. They settle on the following: teaching assistants are based in one class but work across multiple classes to support the children that need help the most.
>
> Knowing that this model is the only affordable one, Helen and her team set about mapping out where teaching assistants might be deployed and how they can minimise their movement between classes as much as possible, having some teaching assistants allocated for EYFS, key stage 1 and key stage 2. Even though they are taking time to think this through now, it is not the solution. Helen also leads the discussion on how they will involve all their colleagues in designing a model that minimises movement but provides the right support where it is needed.

Validating new beliefs and assumptions

The third stage of Schein's model for established leaders to bring about improvement involves validating the new beliefs. Through experiencing success, colleagues need to see that the changes they have made are the right ones. This stage is where the collective beliefs and assumptions will actually evolve. In this example, the success will need to be recognised in relation to target beliefs and assumptions – that the school is operating financially responsibly and that the right support is there for the children who need it the most.

Understand the present

Each chapter in Part 2 invited the reader to develop hidden knowledge of their own school in relation to:

- Building psychological safety, sharing vulnerability and establishing purpose
- Leaders' expectations and biases
- Autonomy, mastery and purpose as the drivers for motivation
- Relational trust

It is this process that the established leader will need to keep on top of in order to deeply understand the present – a prerequisite for making the right choice of goal. In the example, Helen is able to plan for the change because she already knows her colleagues' underlying assumptions about how teaching assistants should be used. It could have gone wrong though. Helen could quite easily have simply mandated that the teaching assistant model was changing because of financial reasons. But this would likely have had a negative influence on climate if colleagues were not involved in solving a problem that affects all of them in their day-to-day school experiences. Had she done this, Helen would not have engaged with her colleagues' theories of action, instead bypassing them completely.

Fortunately, she didn't do this. She engaged with her leadership teams' theories of action and together they planned for how they would engage with others to solve the problem.

Choose the right problem

Remember, despite the importance of school culture, trying to change it directly is futile. Culture change needs to happen through addressing education-specific problems to have meaning because collective actions and beliefs (culture) will be influencing how the problem manifests.

Viviane Robinson suggests a four-part process for engaging with colleagues' theories of action:

- Agree on the problem to be solved
- Inquire into the relevant theory of action
- Evaluate the relative merit of the current and alternative theories of action
- Implement and monitor a new, sufficiently shared theory of action

Example

Helen sets up a meeting with the teachers and a separate meeting with the teaching assistants. She knows that this is not ideal but cannot get the whole group together until the next INSET day. The teacher meeting happens first. Helen explains that the team has a problem and that their help is needed to find solutions: 'Our school has always

> worked on the model of having a teaching assistant in every class and we have always had amazing teaching assistants that make an incredible difference to what children learn. However, you must have noticed that class sizes have been getting smaller as we suffer from the dip in the local birth rate. Our funding is determined by the number of children we have, so fewer children mean less income. I'm afraid to say that when Ismael and Priya retire in the summer, we will not be able to replace them'. Helen lets that message sink in before continuing: 'We have to find an alternative way of working because we can no longer be a school that has a teaching assistant for every class. We have 14 classes but, from September, we will only be able to afford 12 teaching assistants'.
>
> Helen then leads a discussion where colleagues have the opportunity to ask questions and offer solutions. When solutions are offered, the leadership team explains the logistics of how some of the models might work in practice, having mapped them out in their leadership meeting. They do it from a perspective of sharing information and Helen periodically invites opinion about what they think the best solution is.
>
> Later that week, Helen meets with the teaching assistants and explains the problem in a similar way. She adds another detail, specific to these colleagues: 'And this means that, although we will still have a base, many of us will need to work across multiple classes'.
>
> Again, Helen leads a discussion where colleagues have the opportunity to ask questions and make suggestions, with the leadership team providing concrete examples when suggestions are made.

In our example, Helen:

- Presents the team with the problem to be solved (an affordable model for teaching assistant deployment) and seeks ways to solve the problem

- Inquires into the relevant theories of action (she may not have done it at the time but, knowing her team well, she just needs to confirm that this is still the case)

- Involves the team in evaluating the relative merit of the current and alternative theories of action

Design the future

With a clear understanding of the present, the next stage is to design the future. It can be tempting to start with describing culture in terms that are too vague, such as wanting everyone to feel psychologically safe, or for everyone to feel autonomy and flow, or for everyone to have high levels of trust, but remember that these are the results of school culture – the climate that exists because of how everyone behaves. They are desirable, but not helpful, in mapping out how to achieve them.

It can also be tempting to start with describing some generic ways of behaving, such as wanting everyone to share their vulnerabilities or for leaders to notice their biases or communicate a clear purpose. Again, these are desirable but cannot be divorced from the process of solving problems. To help colleagues to modify behaviours, desirable behaviours need to be concrete, exemplified in the tackling of a problem.

So, leaders might then start to list the specific behaviours that are required to tackle the given problem. In our example, the problem is designing an affordable model for the deployment of teaching assistants.

Example

Helen meets with the teachers and the teaching assistants on the INSET day and sets about clarifying a solution to the problem as a result of the previous meetings. They come up with a list:

- Children with EHCPs must have their legal requirement for additional support fulfilled
- Children in the younger years are prioritised over children in the older years
- Teaching assistants work across a maximum of two year groups
- Teaching assistants are based with the least experienced teachers
- Year leaders regularly discuss deployment with each other and request changes when needed for specific activities or for specific children

This discussion is vital. Not only do the team agree on what determines how teaching assistants are deployed, the discussion itself firms up the shared beliefs of the group.

Prioritise aligning beliefs and values

This is much more than a moment standing in front of colleagues and it is much more than the examples given so far in this chapter. It is done daily, through all sorts of interactions with different colleagues:

- Keep talking about beliefs and assumptions – ask what others think and tell others what you think, looking for common ground.
- Get to know individuals' beliefs and assumptions – build up a picture of what each person values and what drives their behaviour.
- Notice language that contradicts your beliefs and assumptions – challenge its use and provide alternatives.

- Notice practices that contradict your beliefs and assumptions – ask why these practices exist and point out that they contradict your beliefs.

The importance of aligning beliefs and values cannot be underestimated. Doing so provides the foundation for good implementation. It can't be rushed.

> **Example**
>
> A teacher in year 5 (Manny) comes to Helen feeling frustrated. He feels as if he cannot support all the children in his class because he hasn't got a teaching assistant. Helen recognises the language that Manny is using and it reveals a belief that still persists from when every class did have a teaching assistant.
>
> Helen wants to explore this belief before looking at a solution: 'What do you mean by not having a teaching assistant?'
>
> Manny explains that, in year 5, they now share a teaching assistant, but she spends more time in the other class.
>
> Helen digs deeper: 'Okay, can you tell me about how your team has timetabled teaching assistant support?'
>
> Manny looks a little unsure and says that he can't remember, but she's never in his class and he has some children that are struggling.
>
> Helen takes the opportunity to find some common ground: 'Well, if there are children that are struggling, I agree that we need to get them the right support. What support do they need?'
>
> Manny gives this some thought and talks about how maths lessons are difficult because he has two children that have much weaker prior knowledge and need him to work with them, which means that he doesn't really get the chance to support any other children.
>
> Helen checks that she has understood: 'So, am I right in thinking that another pair of hands might be helpful in maths lessons? What about other subjects?'
>
> Manny takes a minute and says that it is not so much of an issue in other subjects, that the gap just seems wider in maths.
>
> Helen makes the most of this opportunity to reinforce desired ways of working: 'That's good that it is working better in other subjects. Have you spoken to the rest of your team about timetabling teaching assistant support for your maths lessons?'
>
> Manny explains that he mentioned it once, but everyone has maths at the same time and wants teaching assistant support. He pauses, then suggests that they could change the timetable around so that they have maths at different times.

Prioritise psychological safety

The established leader must understand that the process of aligning beliefs and values, particularly when it comes to challenging or questioning underlying assumptions, will likely create anxiety and defensiveness. Everyone needs stability but, to bring about educational improvement, this sort of challenge and questioning is necessary. The way that it is done makes a significant difference to the climate, though. Chapter 4 described some of the strategies for building safety, summarised here:

- Show warmth and kindness in every interaction
- Give good eye contact
- Engage in frequent, energetic exchanges
- Close physical proximity (but not too close)
- Prevent interruptions
- Eat together
- Encourage humour and laughter
- Treat individuals as unique and valued
- Give small attentive courtesies
- Show that you care
- Make mixing happen
- Ask questions to draw others out
- Celebrate the humblest of tasks
- Narrate others' role in the future
- Create connections between people

Closely related to psychological safety is the importance of leaders sharing their vulnerability. Chapter 4 described some of the strategies for sharing vulnerability, summarised here:

- Seek feedback
- Face uncomfortable truths head on
- Debrief decision-making

Schein's work on organisational culture also outlines strategies to build psychological safety and has these to add:

Strategy	Example
Present a compelling positive vision – we'll be better if we learn the new way of thinking/working	Helen talks excitedly about the opportunity that has arisen in changing how teaching assistants are deployed, particularly about targeting the children that need the most help so that support can be tailored and more specific. She seeks out and uses examples of how some teaching assistants are specialising in supporting a particular need, such as early mathematical development, and how they are feeling more proficient in helping children.
Provide formal training in the new way of thinking/working	Helen keeps teaching assistant deployment on the agenda for leadership meetings, with phase leaders to support them in working through decisions about how to deploy teaching assistants. She also organises regular and specific training for teaching assistants on supporting the most common needs in the school: reading fluency, early mathematical development and emotional support.
Involve people in how to access informal training	Helen knows that the formal training will not be enough to bring about improvement. She knows that teachers are going to need to experience success using these strategies for them to become embedded (indeed that she should only work towards embedding them if they bring about success). She also knows that the financial goal is probably not the one that will mean the most to the children. She knows that she needs to emphasis the goal of children getting the right support and that teaching assistants are just one form of support. She and the leadership team set about looking for examples of well-organised classrooms, great explanations and skilful scaffolding, all of which would help to support the children that need it the most. She encourages colleagues to watch each other and use the shared experience for conversations about supporting children to succeed. She makes sure that each colleague has the opportunity to do so.

Strategy	Example
Create space and time to practice – give time, resources, coaching and feedback	Helen resists the urge to observe lessons. She knows that she can learn enough about how the flexible deployment of teaching assistants is going through conversations aggregated from the experiences of different leaders. Helen keeps asking: 'What do you need that you don't already have that will help with supporting the children that need it the most?' One thing comes up for teachers. Many feel that the curriculum is too full of content and that they are under pressure to cover the curriculum and are sometimes moving on through topics before all the children have understood.
Create support groups where problems can be discussed	Helen knows that colleagues will come across difficulties and wants to create a forum where problem solving can be collaborative. She arranges for a weekly teaching assistant meeting where they can meet – sometimes with Helen, sometimes without – to discuss strategies that have been useful. One common theme is getting used to the different expectations that each teacher has and their different ways of working.

Teach your school how to perceive, think, feel and behave

Schein described tools that leaders can use to teach their organisations to perceive, think, feel and behave. An established leader will have to carefully manage the first six (what Schein calls the primary mechanisms), carrying them all out simultaneously and ensuring consistency of message. But they will also have to recognise the power of the secondary mechanisms because, in a midlife school, these mechanisms will be a deeply embedded part of the culture. They are harder for a leader to control than the first six, but control them they must if they are to bring about improvement and a shift in beliefs and assumptions.

What to pay attention to

The things that leaders notice and comment on become the things that others think leaders value and they will often adjust their behaviour accordingly. Leaders' attention is also revealed through what they decide to measure, control or reward. The implication for leaders is that they must be deliberate and systematic in what they pay attention to in order to influence the behaviours of others. In the examples above, Helen systematically pays attention to supporting children to be successful in different ways in lots of different interactions, clearly communicating what she believes to be important. A common mistake is for leaders to launch an initiative and then not systematically follow it up with appropriate attention.

Helen could have declared victory too soon after the early work on organising new working patterns for teaching assistants and spent more of her time on finance, risk assessments or behaviour. She will undoubtedly have had to pay attention to those things, but the key point is that she did not let them distract her from continued attention to the main issue, for she knew that if her attention appeared to wane, then so would her colleagues'. Not paying sustained attention to priorities creates a vacuum where colleagues will spend time and energy trying to figure out what leaders want. This risks the creation of multiple subcultures where different groups do different things because of the different inferences they have made. A lack of consistency here prevents the primary mechanisms from reinforcing each other.

This can also be exacerbated by paying attention to too many things – if everything is important, then nothing is. Leaders must therefore be careful about what to not pay attention to. It can be equally powerful in reinforcing key messages.

Example

Throughout the work on teaching assistant redeployment, Helen deliberately did not bring up administrative tasks such as photocopying because she wants to make sure that colleagues don't perceive this to be something of importance. She is prepared to address it when it comes up, though, because she knows that the existing culture is for some teaching assistants to spend more time out of the classroom changing books, doing displays or photocopying than working with children. The question comes up after a week or so – one teacher brings up the issue of photocopying and other jobs around the classroom when they do not have a teaching assistant. The next time the team meet together, Helen brings it up: 'I've had a question about administrative tasks. I know that when we had a teaching assistant in every class, these tasks were covered, but I also know how much time they took away from actually working with children. Of course, they still need doing, but we need to look for better, more efficient ways to keep everyone focused on supporting children while getting important administration done'. Whenever Helen is in a classroom, she deliberately never brings up displays, only discussing the extent to which children are being supported. When she finds others paying attention to how long it is taking to photocopy, she gently questions whether it is necessary or whether they could plan ahead and get it done in bulk at a specific point in the week.

How to react to critical incidents

A critical incident is anything that is perceived to be critical. For an established leader, this might be, for example:

- An Ofsted inspection

- An incident leading to an exclusion
- A resignation
- Poor performance on statutory assessment
- An outbreak of illness
- A necessary school closure

The example that Helen is dealing with in her school regarding teaching assistant deployment probably counts as a critical incident and the important thing for leaders to understand and act on is the likely increase in anxiety that many colleagues will experience. The main priority when reacting to critical incidents must be psychological safety.

How to allocate resources

The way that leaders allocate resources demonstrates what they value. These might be physical resources or they might be how people are deployed.

> **Example**
>
> Helen, a headteacher prioritising a necessary new way of deploying teaching assistants, knows the power of cultural artifacts in influencing what colleagues do. Part of the plan is to alleviate some of the pressure on administrative tasks. Helen decides to investigate whether there is any scope for paying one or two teaching assistants for a few extra hours per week to carry out administrative tasks such as photocopying. It would be a small financial cost, but the benefit to teachers (who would be content that what they needed was being done) and to children (more time for support available from teaching assistants who wouldn't be doing this during the day) seems to be worth it. Helen decides to allocate several hundred pounds to fund this for a term to see if it makes a difference.

Deliberate role modelling, teaching and coaching

The leader is the main role model for the school, year groups or phase. Everything that leaders do – from what they pay attention to to the energy and interactions that they have – has a strong influence on culture.

> **Example**
>
> Helen knows that she needs credibility in the eyes of her colleagues. She knows that she is asking her team to take risks in trying new ways of working and she needs to show that she is up to that challenge too. She wants to create a culture where colleagues ask for feedback and are comfortable having others in the room while they teach as a source of feedback. By arranging with each teacher in advance, she teaches each class without teaching assistant support and seeks feedback from each teacher about what worked well and what could have been better.

How to allocate rewards and status

Rewards available to established leaders are, first and foremost, the interactions that they have. Change brings with it opportunity and there will certainly be colleagues who seek to make a difference here and now who also have ambitions for future leadership themselves. A change in culture in the solving of a specific problem creates the opportunity for colleagues to excel and develop their expertise and with this comes status.

> **Example**
>
> During her regular conversations and walks of the school, Helen finds a bright spot in year 6. The least advantaged children seem to be successful; they use carefully planned scaffolds that the teacher (Ravi) gradually removes. Ravi explains concepts in small steps and runs an incredibly organised classroom where every child knows what is expected of them; she aims for high standards. Helen decides to spotlight this success in a number of ways. First, she directs other colleagues to talk to Ravi and to arrange to see her teaching. Then, during a training session where the team is reviewing strategies for ensuring that children get the right support, Helen asks Ravi to talk through an example of how she scaffolds mathematical tasks for children that need it. At the end, Helen once again encourages others to chat to Ravi and arrange to see what she does in action.

Recruitment, promotion and performance management

The team that leaders assemble has the potential to reinforce school culture. There is a balance that leaders should try to achieve here, though. While it may be useful to have a team that shares beliefs, values and assumptions, it is also important to encourage alternative points of view to avoid creating an echo chamber.

> **Example**
>
> Helen (who has been working on the redeployment of teaching assistants to best support children) receives a resignation from a teacher who has secured a promotion elsewhere and needs to recruit a replacement. When she shows potential candidates around, she talks about their model of deploying teaching assistants and introduces them to key people such as Ravi from the previous example, encouraging them to talk about supporting children to succeed through scaffolding. The interview process includes teaching a maths lesson without a teaching assistant and some of the questions are designed to find out what the candidates' underlying assumptions about teaching assistant support are in order to see the extent of a match between each candidate and the emerging culture. Helen also creates opportunities on the interview day for other colleagues to get to know the candidates because she knows that the more people she can get opinions from about which candidate is the best fit, the more valid her decision will be. This also helps to maintain trust with her team, as she is asking their opinion on an important matter such as recruitment.

The secondary mechanisms

For an established leader in a midlife school, the secondary mechanisms become primary mechanisms in the influence that they have over school culture. They can be a lot harder for leaders to control and, if they are inconsistent with the primary mechanisms, can cause conflict that will threaten the leader's improvement agenda and the climate.

Organisational design and structure

> **Example**
>
> Navroop is a headteacher of a school that has recently been judged as requiring improvement. The areas for improvement are centred around curriculum development and there is a lot of work to be done to improve the curriculum offer. The school has a healthy surplus, so Navroop makes a suggestion to the chair of governors. The current structure involves the deputy headteacher, who leads on curriculum development but also teaches for two days per week. Navroop proposes that the school employ a part-time teacher on a fixed-term contract for a year to take this responsibility away from the deputy headteacher, enabling them to have more time for the necessary curriculum development work. It is not affordable permanently, but, in the short term, it can be covered by the surplus and the structure can return to normal after a year of intensive work.

School systems and procedures

If the established leaders do not design and maintain school systems, it opens the door to inconsistencies in the culture and any improvement message that the leaders want to broadcast can be weakened. In designing and adapting these systems, the goal is to keep shared beliefs at the forefront of decision-making and bring stability, consistency and, ultimately, psychological safety.

> **Example**
>
> Helen wants systems to reinforce the beliefs and assumptions about getting the right support for children with fewer teaching assistants. Together with her leadership team, she comes up with the following:
>
> - Phase leaders to ensure that each teaching assistant has a timetable of which class they are supporting, for which subject (and which children). Timetable reviewed half termly at least.
> - Phase leaders to ensure that each teacher has a timetable detailing when they will have teaching assistant support and for which subject. Teachers are expected to specifically direct teaching assistants to work with specific children on specific tasks.
> - Teachers to be responsible for communicating with teaching assistants in advance what is expected of them.
> - Photocopying is not to be done by teaching assistants during school hours. Teachers can email what they would like to the photocopying email address (including the date when it is needed) and this will be picked up by the teaching assistants responsible for this out of school hours.
> - At every team meeting, phase leaders to discuss any proposed amendments to teaching assistant deployment.

Design of physical space and buildings

Schools often have limited scope to change physical space, with building work a luxury only afforded in instances of major repairs, expansion or, in even rarer cases, relocation or rebuilding. What leaders can have control over, though, is how those spaces are looked after. An example that aligns with Helen's story of changing the deployment of teaching assistants does not quite fit, so this mechanism might be better explained with a non-example where there are obvious contradictions between this and other mechanisms.

> **Non-example**
>
> Ciaran is the deputy headteacher and responsible for the quality of teaching. One of the initiatives that he is developing is the understanding of cognitive load theory among teachers, focusing on the idea that working memory can easily be overloaded by a number of environmental factors. Teachers have been working on the clarity of their explanations and the sequencing of curriculum content to avoid cognitive overload for children, but Ciaran has noticed that there is one part of school life that quite obviously contradicts these messages – the school environment itself. Classroom walls are covered with display boards, working walls, posters and children's work. There is almost no empty space on walls and the same is true for shared space such as corridors. Added to this, a lot of the school seems messy and disorganised.

Stories and myths about key people and events

There are two elements to this. The first is more controllable by leaders, who can broadcast their vision for the future. In every communication leaders have with teachers, with parents, with children and the wider community, they should talk their desired culture into existence. Filling the windscreen with stories can help to drive behaviour by providing examples of what leaders value. But there is a less controllable element to this, too, in the stories that others tell of leaders. Considering that every action and every word is analysed by colleagues, how leaders treat others and how they deal with situations become the stories that are told. To increase the likelihood of such stories being desirable, leaders must of course always act with integrity – alignment with what leaders say is important and they have to be visible, making it their business to have multiple interactions daily in pursuit of common goals.

> **Example**
>
> One of the ways that Helen builds psychological safety into her project to change how teaching assistants are deployed is to show her vulnerability. She does this by teaching every class without a teaching assistant and seeking feedback on how well she supports the children that need it the most. Because she does this in every class, it is a topic of conversation between colleagues based on a shared experience. One of the stories that reaches most colleagues is about her endeavours in year 4. The lesson does not go particularly well and, when Helen asks for feedback, she is told that her explanation wasn't particularly clear and, as a result, some children were a little unclear on what they were expected to do. This becomes a story that is told, but the important part is what happens next. Helen, keen to show that she values the feedback, asks to go back to that

> same class to act on the feedback given. The teacher is a little surprised because this is more than what Helen had committed to doing, but she respects Helen for it. It is this final part of the story that becomes an important element of what is shared because it shows Helen's dedication to getting it right.

Formal mission statements, charters and ethical code

Most schools have these aims, mottos or vision statements in some form or other and Chapter 3 describes a model for school improvement that can help leaders to clarify their thinking around strategic direction. However, these cannot be viewed as a way for leaders to define culture when culture is the collective beliefs, assumptions and behaviours of the team. All they provide is a focus for the team to help guide decision-making and solve problems. They are brought to life by the problem solving engaged in by leaders, keeping them focused on desired outcomes and behaving in line with commonly agreed values.

Chapter summary

- The existing leader will need to create the motivation for change to address a well-established culture – colleagues need to see for themselves that change is necessary.
- Once this is the case, it is important to align collective beliefs and assumptions, which may have evolved differently in different subgroups in an established culture.
- Colleagues will need to see that new ways of working are successful and attribute this success to those new ways of working.
- Existing leaders need to take time to make sure that they understand the present by inquiring into the culture and climate of the school.
- But this cannot be done generally. This knowledge building needs to be based around specific problems. Doing so will help the existing leader to choose the right problem to focus on.
- Existing leaders need to design the future with the team – to set the strategic direction so that colleagues understand where they're going and why.

- Existing leaders ought to prioritise aligning colleagues' beliefs and values.
- Psychological safety will always be at risk when the existing leader instigates change, so leaders must understand and prioritise it.
- Existing leaders can use the school's established systems to keep the new shared beliefs and practices at the forefront of colleagues' minds.

Why measuring culture is futile and evaluating it is not much better

Introduction

School accountability systems are baked into leaders' practice. It is common to seek to make judgements on how good their practices are and essentially how good their culture is. But just because they are common, it doesn't mean they are accurate or it is right for leaders to spend their time measuring and evaluating. This chapter explains the reasons why leaders shouldn't try to measure culture and why judgements on how good their culture is are unlikely to be accurate. It proposes a different way of working: inquiry over measurement, knowledge building over judgement.

The problem with measurement and evaluation

Measurement and evaluation are common in schools, but their existence is not proof of their usefulness. So many interactions between so many rather unpredictable individuals (not least children) contribute to incredible complexity and one thing is certain – it is almost impossible to directly link cause and effect.

> **Example**
>
> This year, attainment in reading at the end of KS2 is higher compared to the previous academic year. The headteacher, Kim, and her senior leadership sit down to debrief, thinking through the reasons for it, and they come up with this list:
>
> - It is because of the now 'research informed' reading strategy.
> - It is because of better attendance.
> - It is because the children read better books over the course of year 6.
> - It is because behaviour was better.

> - It is because there were different teachers to last year in year 6.
> - It is because of the relative starting points of the two cohorts.
> - It is because this cohort had consistent teachers all the way through key stage 2 whereas the previous cohort didn't.
>
> Each leader who advocated a particular reason was adamant that theirs was the key, while others dismissed them in favour of their own.

The truth is that it will have been a combination of all these reasons and more, each playing minor and major roles at different points in time.

If there is one leadership behaviour that underestimates complexity it is making bold claims attributing cause and effect. Nonetheless, it is an understandable and natural attempt to make sense of phenomena by imposing some sort of order on the chaos of school life. Kim and her leadership team in the example given are suffering from the illusion of explanatory depth, where they think they understand more than they actually do, characterised by assigning cause to effect, and it is an illusion that we are all susceptible to.

Gathering quantitative or qualitative information in order to evaluate school culture or climate is ingrained in our schools and it is well worth challenging these orthodoxies. Leaders need to be wary of the shortcomings of measuring complex systems. Muller warns of the tyranny of metrics[1]:

- Avoid using numerical indicators
- Not everything that matters is measurable
- Not everything that is measurable matters
- The more a metric is used to make decisions, the more it will be gamed
- Measurement is not an alternative to judgement

Avoid using numerical indicators

The argument for metrics is that, by reducing complex information to percentages of respondents on a survey, points on a scale or numerical values, comparisons within and between schools are easier and more easily understood and therefore useful to hold leaders to account. This is fundamentally flawed. Although this simplification of information makes it comparable, what is lost is history, context and meaning:

> Caveats and ambiguities are peeled away, giving the illusion of certainty and transparency.[1]

The illusion of certainty is a problem for school leaders because it oversimplifies complex problems. Complexity cannot be measured. Just as a mean average summarises a range of numbers, any metric that leaders select merely represents the complex inaccurately.

Not everything that matters is measurable

Culture matters, but, as we have seen, culture is the collective beliefs and assumptions that influence espoused values and create cultural artifacts. Measuring one person's beliefs, assumptions and behaviours is impossible enough, let alone doing so for the collective beliefs and behaviours of a large group.

Climate matters too and leaders might feel the need to measure an element of it such as staff wellbeing. A broad concept like this cannot be measured, of course, so the only way of doing so would be to measure proxies, such as responses to survey questions, sickness absence or staff retention data. These proxies, and any others that aim to measure wellbeing, can only represent a small sample of the entire domain and that is assuming they are even valid proxies. Further, the very attempts at measuring wellbeing can result in a negative influence on it. Consider a staff survey that contains questions designed to evaluate how colleagues feel about working practices. Wellbeing and workload are two sides of the same coin, so additional work, such as a long survey to complete, can have a negative effect on staff wellbeing.

The complexity only increases from here, though. Perceptions of workload matter more than actual time spent working and if colleagues knew that their survey contributions were genuinely listened to and resulted in improvement, then the time spent completing it would be worthwhile. Conversely, if colleagues considered the survey to be a token gesture that would never result in change, then the time spent completing it would be considered wasted. When completing a survey, some colleagues may feel reluctant to express negative opinions, even if it were anonymous, for fear of repercussions, further affecting wellbeing.

The vicious circle between metrics and trust

The way in which evaluation is carried out will have consequences throughout the complex school system. The demand for measured accountability waxes as trust wanes. A lack of trust leads to more metrics and more metrics leads to less reliance on judgement.

Not everything that can be measured matters

The path of least resistance is to collect information on things that are easy to measure. Attendance and sickness absence, for example, are absolute; colleagues are either at work or they are not. Staff turnover is also absolute. Data can be gathered on how many colleagues leave each year. However, just because it is easy to measure doesn't mean that the data is useful.

The more a metric is used to make decisions, the more it will be gamed

A significant risk of reducing complex information to a metric is how that information is used by leaders and how colleagues behave regarding the collection of required data. If high stakes decisions are based on metrics, there is always the chance that they have been manipulated in order to gain reward or avoid negative consequences. If a metric becomes high stakes, once-noble goals are easily displaced as effort is diverted to what gets measured. A culture of curriculum narrowing is a prime example of this towards the end of key stage 2. SATs assess elements of English and maths, while other subjects are not assessed at all. When so much rides on good results, it is obvious why some leaders and teachers prioritise English and maths at the expense of a broad and balanced curriculum.

The flaw of measuring inputs not outcomes

There's one particular misconception around impact – that it is not the same as actions.

> **Example**
>
> A headteacher is sitting across the table from governors, their MAT line manager or an HMI who ask what progress the school has made towards the areas for improvement published in the most recent Ofsted report from last year's inspection. The headteacher, naturally, knows exactly what those areas for improvement are and, regarding the one that referenced a need to improve behaviour (particularly around low-level disruption), responds by telling their interviewer that senior colleagues have attended behaviour training provided by the local authority. The headteacher has given no consideration to how well colleagues have implemented any strategies developed as a result of the work with the local authority's behaviour adviser or indeed whether behaviour is actually any better than it was at the time of the previous inspection.

In this example, the headteacher emphasises what he has done. These actions might well have been important in improving behaviour, but he did not articulate the change in culture that his actions led to, or indeed the climate.

Measurement is not an alternative to judgement

Muller's warnings about the tyranny of metrics will resonate with school leaders in an education system that has so many accountability mechanisms. Those responsible for governance often want to know if schools are getting better and because they are not in a position to experience school culture and climate for themselves, they (or the school leaders) devise ways of distilling complex behaviours and feelings into measurements in order to feel as if they have a grasp of how the school (or schools) are doing. But, as Muller concludes, measurement demands judgement:

- Whether to measure culture and climate
- What to measure
- How to evaluate the significance of what's been measured
- Whether rewards or penalties will be attached to the results
- To whom to make the measurements available

Can culture and climate be measured or evaluated?

Culture cannot be measured or evaluated in its entirety because it is so vast. The best that leaders can hope for is to look into culture and climate in relation to a specific problem. This has been the focus of the examples of how a new leader (Chapter 8) and an established leader (Chapter 9) might go about influencing culture and climate.

As we have seen, measuring or evaluating aspects of school life cannot be done with an acceptable level of reliability and, as such, any judgements that leaders might make are subject to issues of validity. Some leaders might then seek external viewpoints on culture and climate, but this is even harder for an outsider to determine. At best they might notice the most superficial level of culture and climate – the artifacts. And because they cannot possibly tell if collective ways of working are having a positive impact or not, all they can do is judge within their own frame of reference – whether they approve of the practices they are seeing. Such practices provide only an illusion of certainty about how good the culture and climate are.

Maybe, then, a better way of working would be to compare what has been seen at different points in time. Leaders could seek out whether what teachers are doing now is better than what they were doing before, or whether colleagues feel better about elements of climate (such as autonomy, purpose, psychological safety, etc.)

now than they did before. The same problem persists, though, in that judgements in the first place are unlikely to be accurate and reliable.

As we have seen throughout this book, a strong culture and a positive climate are reliant on (among many things) a clear direction and purpose from leaders. If leaders have designed the future ideal well, then perhaps they might be able to compare what they see now with that ideal. This seems more palatable than the previous options, but it is flawed for two reasons. The first is the risk of confirmation bias.

> **Example**
>
> Jen has been working on a clear vision for the future regarding improving outcomes for children and part of this vision is increased collaboration between teachers. When she started in post, teachers worked on their own to plan and reflect on lessons and Jen introduced PPA time for year teams together to encourage collaboration. Jen has a deeply held assumption that planning together is an important driver in ensuring better sequences of lessons.
>
> Months later, Jen is reflecting on how far the school has come towards realising this vision and this conversation is part of her appraisal review. Jen knows that teachers are meeting together during PPA and describes this as a successful culture change to her line manager.

In this example, Jen knows that, superficially, teachers have PPA at the same time and makes the assumption that this is resulting in improved collaboration. She may well miss the fact that the reality of these meetings is that teaching teams talk very little, working more alongside each other than with each other. She sees a situation that resonates with her as a step in the right direction towards the desired culture, but the reality may not be what she thinks it is.

The second reason why comparing now and a future ideal is flawed is that there is nothing to guarantee that the vision of the future culture is even effective. Leaders might have an idea of what works well from their own prior experiences, from research or from the practices of other schools. If practices have been successful, however, then it will not have been solely the practices that made the difference but the complex interplay between those practices and the shared beliefs and assumptions of the team. The way that practices are implemented can make or break their effectiveness, which is why, in education, we have the phenomenon that two schools can choose the same ways of working but get completely different results and why we have the proverb that everything works somewhere but nothing works everywhere.

Surely leaders can tell if culture or climate is *not* good?

What about making a judgement when something is not good? It is arguably easier to judge when practice is poor given that this scenario likely involves quite obvious indicators, such as:

- Apathy on colleagues' part
- Open hostility between colleagues
- Poor behaviour going unaddressed
- Children routinely not understanding work or getting appropriate support

If these cultural artifacts are present, then it simply makes it easier for leaders to identify a problem that needs solving and to explore possible solutions.

A shift from evaluating to inquiring about culture and climate

If measurement and evaluation are so deeply flawed, then what? Leaders have to do something, surely, otherwise they are running their schools and seeking improvement while fumbling in the dark. Perhaps what is needed is a shift. A shift from metrics and evaluation to a spirit of inquiry where leaders seek to understand as much of the full complexity of their culture and climate as possible rather than judge it.

The suggestions for developing hidden knowledge at the end of each chapter in Part 2 are designed for this very purpose. This is building knowledge. Leaders who build knowledge of their school culture and climate are in a much stronger position to bring about improvement than those who seek to judge in an environment where their future in their job often relies on those judgements to be good and backed up externally. Where judgements prevail, as Muller has described, gaming is not far behind, and gaming is a threat to actual improvement.

Building knowledge through inquiry without judgement is about seeking an accurate picture so that better decisions can be made, about skilfully diagnosing problems and addressing the necessary issues.

How can leaders inquire into culture?

The profession now has more shared knowledge than ever at its fingertips and this continues to be refined. This shared knowledge is there to be grasped by leaders and applied in their schools, but doing so is only advisable when leaders have a true understanding of their own school culture:

- What problem do they need to solve? And what are their new proposed ways of working?

- What are the visible cultural artifacts in their school related to this problem?

- What are the espoused values related to this problem? What do they say is important?

- What are their underlying beliefs and assumptions related to this problem?

- Are these beliefs and assumptions an aid to their proposed new ways of working on the problem or a hindrance?

Discussion seems the most appropriate way to get to the root of cultural inquiry because it is the determination of underlying beliefs and assumptions that provides leaders with the most useful information with which to plan improvement. And because culture is the collective beliefs and assumptions of the group, it is discussion with groups rather than individuals that should yield useful information for leaders.

The elements of climate described in Part 2 of this book could all be the subject of data collection, but, just like enquiring into culture, it needs to be based around the solving of a problem rather than inquiring into climate in its entirety. And it fits right in with the second step detailed above – what are the visible artifacts in a leader's school that relate to this problem? These elements are the experiences of the team, so it is colleagues' perception of them that could be captured to provide an insight. The design of each chapter in Part 2 includes a section of prompts and questions that leaders can use to inquire into school climate for the particular problem they are inquiring into.

Further, such inquiry relies on the knowledge of the person or people doing it – if they do not fully understand how relational trust, for example, is built and maintained, they will not be able to effectively find out information related to it, hence the importance of knowledge building about concepts involved in culture and climate.

While a combination of observation and group discussions are the most reliable way to inquire into culture and climate, inquiry into school climate does have another option. Surveys could be used where colleagues self-report their feelings of autonomy, belonging or mastery, etc. Common in schools is the annual survey that individuals complete, but aggregating individual perceptions is perhaps not the same as collecting group perceptions. Arguably, it might be more beneficial for teams to complete a survey together to represent the group, allowing space for elaboration and explanation if there are differing viewpoints. There are some important considerations for leaders when writing surveys, exemplified by this question: *To what extent do you feel that you have autonomy?*

Question design

How questions are phrased can significantly influence the responses received. The example question might be very hard to answer because, as described in Chapter 6, there are different elements to autonomy. Naturally, colleagues will have different levels of autonomy over different aspects of their working conditions. Leaders need to focus in on which aspect(s) of autonomy they really want to know about, related to the problem they intend to tackle, therefore the question would be far more useful if it enquired into the perception of autonomy in a specific area of school life, such as: *To what extent do you feel that you have autonomy over your professional development?*

Scaling

To generate trend data, surveys often use scaling and the choice of scale is important. Take the question: *To what extent do you feel that you have autonomy over your professional development?* The scale could have three parts to it:

- None
- Some
- Full

In this case, because the first and last options are absolute, they are unlikely to be how most colleagues would perceive their autonomy and leaders would be likely to get most responses in the middle option. Full autonomy over professional development might not even be possible, as leaders will need to guide what colleagues work on to align with school priorities. The options could be rephrased:

- Very little
- Some
- Lots

Even so, the Goldilocks trap is still a risk and still might not result in any useful information. An odd number of options will inevitably have a middle, neutral choice, therefore maybe four options would be better in order to find the nuance in colleagues' perceptions:

- Very little
- Some
- Lots

- Full

Asking colleagues to quantify autonomy is still a tricky concept, though, and it might be more useful to switch from this to an agreement scale based on the statement: *We have autonomy over our professional development goals.*

- Strongly agree
- Agree
- Disagree
- Strongly disagree

Phrasing a survey in this way has the advantage of keeping it perception focused rather than trying to quantify something that probably isn't quantifiable. It also gives leaders a chance to make statements about what they feel is important. '*We have autonomy over our professional development goals*' sounds far more purposeful than '*To what extent do you have autonomy over your professional development goals?*'.

Anonymity

Whether a survey is anonymous or not can influence the responses that teachers give. In a model where colleagues put their names to responses, a negative response to a question or statement might be avoided for fear of reprisals if there is little trust. Results would be unreliable in this case. Some colleagues might even just choose the options they think leaders want to hear. Anonymity can go some way to preventing these things from happening and, as has already been described, group completion of surveys provides an element of psychological safety. The downside to anonymity is that, if there are responses that leaders might like to explore or address individually, it becomes impossible using this information alone. Anonymity might make the data more accurate of actual perception, but it also makes it harder to address specific issues.

Timing

The timing of surveying colleagues needs careful consideration in order for the survey to yield the most reliable results. Schools go through cycles of intense and less intense activity, sometimes with parts of a term or academic year packed with a more seasonal workload, such as assessments, reports or extracurricular commitments. Survey responses cannot be evaluated in a bubble – contextual information about conditions at the time of completion need to be taken into account.

Take up

The number of colleagues that respond is important. A majority positive response to the question about autonomy might be pleasing, but if only a third of colleagues answered the question, then it may not be representative of how they all feel. Anonymity makes it impossible to know who has and has not completed the survey. However, group completion of a survey enables all to contribute.

Knowing that what you're aiming for is good enough

A probable response to this model of inquiry and knowledge building over judgement and evaluation is the uneasy feeling of not making judgements – surely leaders have to judge the quality of what is happening in their schools? Well, they already have enough judgement. Ofsted grades and published statutory assessment data bring with them plenty of it, as well as local authority or MAT reviews.

Instead of adding more judgement to the system, the scaffold of whether what leaders are doing is any good can once again be knowledge building. It is leaders' moral imperative to front-load their strategic choices and decision-making with the deliberate curation of formal knowledge, formal knowledge that is essential to tackling the persistent problems of school leadership, some of which is codified in this book but more so around the best that is known about how children learn, what makes great teaching and the elements of effective CPD.

In this instance, the importance of using all that available knowledge to set strategic direction is once more underscored. If sufficient thought, conversation and challenge has gone into identifying the specific problems and designing a future ideal, this can be reassuring for those seeking judgement and there are certainly ways of making this process of setting direction more robust.

The first is the availability and accessibility of formal knowledge of school improvement. The National Professional Qualifications have taken the profession a significant step forward in identifying what leaders should know and know how to do.

The second is ensuring challenge in the process of setting direction by involving multiple people to screen school improvement priorities. The Measures of Effective Teaching project set up by the Gates Foundation[2] found that the *most* reliable form of judging the quality of teaching through observation required multiple observers, multiple observations and rigorous criteria to produce a moderate reliability. The reality of judging lessons through observation has been very far removed from this standard in many, if not all, schools and here lies a parallel with setting school direction.

Perhaps multiple contributors, each meeting the high expectations of having built sufficient domain-specific knowledge of school improvement and setting direction (both formal and hidden), would result in a future ideal that is at least 'good enough'? Let's return to the inquiry model proposed earlier in this chapter:

- What problem do we need to solve? And what are our new proposed ways of working?
- What are the visible cultural artifacts in our school related to this problem?
- What are the espoused values related to this problem? What do we say is important?
- What are our underlying beliefs and assumptions related to this problem?
- Are these beliefs and assumptions an aid to our proposed new ways of working on the problem or a hindrance?

This model is topped and tailed by defining proposed new ways of working. The first prompt to think about this is based on the problem that leaders have noticed, probably relying more so on their formal knowledge, but the last prompt guides leaders towards running these proposed new ways of working through the filter of extensive hidden knowledge, all that leaders have uncovered through inquiry. It is well worth returning to Chapter 3 with this model in mind.

How rubrics fail

Ultimately, even after doing any of this, culture and climate are still complex systems and leaders perhaps delude themselves if they think they can generate an accurate understanding of them, even if they are basing their inquiries around a specific problem. All leaders would be doing, and all they have ever done, is seek to apply a rubric to help them to make sense of the complexity. Greg Ashman skilfully describes how such rubrics fail[3] by explaining that, because of the complexity of a domain such as culture and climate, it is difficult to understand in its entirety. To help leaders' understanding, it is common to develop a rubric, a set of indicators (such as the model for inquiry over judgement described above or the elements of climate described in Part 2 of this book).

Now this second stage of Ashman's model is absolutely necessary for leaders to build knowledge because they need some sort of framework to focus their thinking. But it is what happens next that counts and there are traps to avoid. The trap is that leaders continue to pay attention to just the rubric and not the full complexity of the domain.

Do leaders stay wedded to the rubric, paying attention only to the more easily defined and observable?

Consider the leader that takes a particular shine to the idea of sharing vulnerability. They might engage in deep reflection about their own vulnerability and seek feedback from others. It might become their thing, where they look for it in others and challenge when they don't see it.

Do leaders seek to 'improve' these things, thinking that, by doing so, they're improving school culture and climate?

A leader who has made sharing vulnerability their thing might be able to improve others' vulnerability and make the inference that culture and climate is better as a result of their actions.

Both are flaws in human nature, as we seek to simplify the complex to make sense of it or reassure ourselves that we are making a difference. An alternative is for leaders to zoom back out from the particular rubric that has supported them to tackle a specific problem, fully expecting that, in a complex system, there will be plenty of unintended consequences to the actions that they have taken, not least creating new problems that need their attention. Perhaps, then, the next step is to return to their strategic direction, their future ideal and to start the process of problem solving and diagnosis again with whichever problem takes priority.

Chapter summary

- Schools are complex and it is impossible to disentangle cause and effect.
- Simplifying information to numbers or grades strips out context and meaning, the very elements of it that are useful.
- Judgement and evaluation can have a significant negative impact on trust.
- If information gathered is used for high stakes purposes, that information is at great risk of being gamed.
- Leaders cannot build their knowledge of culture and climate in their entirety because they are so vast and complex. The best that leaders can hope for is to inquire into culture and climate in relation to a specific problem.
- Leaders ought to be wary of confirmation bias if comparing current culture and climate with a future ideal.
- Noticing when culture and climate are *not* good is a lot more straightforward than trying to ascertain *how good* they are.
- This book advocates a shift from metrics and evaluation to a spirit of inquiry where leaders seek to understand as much of the full complexity of their culture and climate as possible rather than judge it.
- Discussion seems the most appropriate way to get to the root of cultural inquiry. The determination of underlying beliefs and assumptions provides leaders with the most useful information with which to plan improvement.
- Discussion with groups rather than individuals yields the most useful information for leaders because they need to know the *collective* beliefs and assumptions.

- Surveys can be improved by requesting group completion.
- Being held to account for a clear strategic direction and having the necessary knowledge to implement it is the antidote to judgement and evaluation.

References

1. Muller, Jerry. (2018). *The tyranny of metrics*. Princeton: Prince University Press.
2. Bill & Melinda Gates Foundation. (2013). 'Measures of effective teaching project releases final research report'. www.gatesfoundation.org/ideas/media-center/press-releases/2013/01/measures-of-effective-teaching-project-releases-final-research-report.
3. Ashman, Greg. (2015). 'Can teaching be given a score?'. https://gregashman.wordpress.com/2015/04/03/can-teaching-be-given-a-score/.

Index

active ingredients 30–1, 73, 74
artifacts 7–8, 10, 13, 14, 44, 62, 146, 147, 150
assumptions 5, 7, 10–12, 19, 25, 26, 30, 66, 71, 103, 104, 109, 113, 121, 124, 125, 127–9, 134, 138–9, 142, 145, 147, 151, 152; *see also* beliefs
attention 60, 62, 63, 65, 67, 69, 105, 116–18, 121, 131–2, 151
autonomy 9, 71–9, 82, 109

beliefs 1, 7, 10, 12–14, 24–6, 30, 62, 64, 103, 104, 109, 110, 112–13, 121, 124, 127–9, 134, 138–9, 142, 145, 147, 151, 152; *see also* assumptions
belonging 2, 40, 44, 56, 60
bias 19, 59, 60, 62, 64, 65, 69, 109, 153
boss competence 86
Bryk, A. 84, 86

complex 1, 13, 18, 24, 27, 107, 142–4, 151–3
complexity 1, 18, 72, 140–2, 146, 151
conflict 85–9, 96, 97, 100
context 5, 6, 19, 22, 23, 25, 40, 103, 141
Coyle, D. 39, 40, 45, 49, 50

domain specific knowledge 2, 16, 18, 19, 23, 36, 54, 150; *see also* knowledge

expectations 2, 59–64, 67–9, 109
expert 1, 2, 12, 17, 19, 25; *see also* expertise

expertise 18, 21, 22, 37, 40, 48, 65, 72, 73, 87; *see also* expert

flourish 14, 85
flow 9, 76–7, 79, 82
formal knowledge 2, 16, 19, 25, 26, 44, 150, 151

Goleman, D. 16–18

headteacher 12, 66–7, 108
hidden knowledge 16, 19, 25, 71, 124–5; *see also* informal knowledge
high performance 21, 22, 39, 56, 57, 60, 64

illusion of certainty 142, 144
informal knowledge 44, 45, 64, 65, 151 *see also* hidden knowledge

knowledge 1, 17, 18, 21, 22, 24, 48, 54, 147; *see also* domain specific knowledge
knowledge building 1, 2, 5, 13, 14, 20, 22, 32, 54, 63, 66, 77, 78, 92–3, 95, 121, 138, 140, 146, 147, 150, 151, 153

marginal gain 56, 60, 104
mastery 9, 71, 76, 77, 82, 109
mental model 16–18, 20, 23, 48, 56, 68, 72, 85
motivation 2, 71, 78, 82, 109

open to learning conversations 46–7

persistent problem 1, 6, 16–18, 22, 24, 36, 150
Pink, D. 71, 76, 77
problem solving 6, 16–18, 21, 110–12, 126, 127, 146, 147
psychological safety 2, 8, 39, 40, 44, 54–7, 105, 109, 114, 121, 129, 136, 139
purpose 9, 24, 28, 39, 49, 54, 55, 57, 58, 71, 72, 77–9, 83, 109, 145
Pygmalion effect 59

Robinson, V. 6–7, 18, 21, 25, 46, 85, 104, 110, 125

Schein, E. 6, 10–11, 62, 103, 105, 107, 108, 115, 116, 122, 123, 130, 131
Sneider, B. 84, 86
strategic direction 2, 21, 24, 25, 32, 33, 49, 72, 75, 89, 121, 138, 145, 150, 153

theory of action 6–7, 109–11, 125, 126
trust 2, 10, 18, 21, 84, 85, 100, 109, 142

values 26–7, 33, 49, 107, 109, 121
vision 21, 25, 29, 49, 115, 130
vulnerability 39, 45, 47, 54, 55, 57, 58, 64–5, 85, 86, 96, 97, 100, 109, 114, 129, 152

Wiliam, D. 11, 26

For Product Safety Concerns and Information please contact our EU representative GPSR@taylorandfrancis.com
Taylor & Francis Verlag GmbH, Kaufingerstraße 24, 80331 München, Germany